Prospects for Peacemaking

Prospects for Peacemaking
A Citizen's Guide to Safer Nuclear Strategy

*edited by Harlan Cleveland
and Lincoln P. Bloomfield*

The MIT Press
Cambridge, Massachusetts
London, England

This volume was prepared in conjunction with "Prospects for Peacemaking: Rethinking National Security and Arms Control," a continuing program of the Hubert H. Humphrey Institute of Public Affairs of the University of Minnesota in cooperation with the Committee for National Security, Honeywell, Inc., and the League of Women Voters of Minnesota.

The Hubert H. Humphrey Institute is open to a diversity of opinions and aspirations. The institute itself does not take positions on issues of public policy. The contents of this book are the responsibility of the authors and the editors.

Hubert H. Humphrey Institute of Public Affairs
University of Minnesota, Humphrey Center
301 19th Avenue South
Minneapolis, Minnesota 55455

This book was set in Baskerville by Graphic Composition, Inc., and printed and bound by Halliday Lithograph in the United States of America.

Library of Congress Cataloging-in-Publication Data

Prospects for peacemaking.

Includes index.
1. Nuclear arms control—United States. 2. Nuclear arms control—Soviet Union. 3. Peace. I. Cleveland, Harlan. II. Bloomfield, Lincoln Palmer, 1920–.
JX1974.7.P767   1987   327.1'72   87–2622
ISBN 0–262–03131–0

Contents

Afterword: Rethinking National Security and Arms Control   *129*
Dean Rusk

Preface: The Minnesota Experiment
Harlan Cleveland

If "war starts in the minds of men," as the framers of the United Nations declared forty years ago, peace also starts in the minds of men—and in the '80s, it seems, especially in the minds of women. In this respect, peace-or-war issues are not all that different from the way U.S. policy is made in other domains.

Whether it is growth policy, or environment policy, or issues about fairness or rights or choice or the social fallout of new technologies, citizen opinion shapes the government's sense of direction. Each of the major shifts of U.S. policy these past four decades has been preceded by a gathering consensus in the U.S. segment of what our Declaration of Independence calls "the general opinion of mankind."

This has been true not only on civil rights and women's status and pollution control; in foreign affairs, it has been equally true of the accommodation with Communist China, the abandonment of our uncertain mission in Vietnam, SALT I and the antiballistic missile treaty, the post-post-Vietnam rebuilding of our military strength under Presidents Carter and Reagan, and President Reagan's turn toward arms control negotiations in his second four-year term of office.

In Minnesota, which has long been hospitable to new ideas, a chance to test and reinforce this kind of citizen-led policymaking presented itself at the beginning of 1984.

The top management and board of Honeywell Inc., a Minneapolis-based maker of control systems that, with 25 percent of its $6 billion-a-year business, is one of the nation's largest defense industries, decided the corporation should be investing in the control as well as the manufacture of weapons. At the same time, the University of Minnesota's Hubert H. Humphrey Institute of Public Affairs was starting an ambitious program of policy research on the future of international governance and the rethinking of basic assumptions about "national security." The Washington-based Committee for National Security was likewise concerned with rethinking arms control policy and impressed with the importance of consulting citizens while doing so. And the lively leadership of the League of Women Voters of Minnesota made a natural partner for a Minnesota experiment in helping citizens reconsider the way Americans think about their safety in a world of nuclear dangers.

These four organizations banded together early in 1984 to conceive and carry out a program funded by Honeywell and managed by the Humphrey Institute. We called the joint venture "Prospects for Peacemaking: Rethinking National Security and Arms Control." The idea was to complete, in a year's time, an urgent and serious effort to rethink the whole subject from scratch.

The process we used was extraordinary: a uniquely interactive dialogue between citizens and experts. The process had three parts, none of which would have worked without the other two.

• A group of citizens covering the whole spectrum of current opinion on national security, arms control, and disarmament policy, who came together frequently to interact with each other and with the specialists.

• A small group of specialists, selected from around the country, with one main qualification in mind: that they be people, some younger and some older, some men and some women, who were least likely to be afflicted with "hardening of the categories."

• A series of public forums to bring the self-educated Minnesota citizens into public dialogue with some of the visible participants in the national debate on national security policy. The way the stage was set for these public forums—the visiting luminaries and the surrogate citizens both on stage and on camera—was designed to illustrate and enhance a dialogue among equals. During the spring of 1984, four two-and-one-half-hour forums were given gavel-to-gavel coverage by public radio and by public television.

After probing for citizen concerns, we met with fifteen specialists chosen for their capacity to think freely, beyond their technical knowledge. We presented to these specialists a set of questions based on the citizen consultations—very different, more fundamental questions than are usually discussed at meetings on national security and arms control.

The specialists turned out to be equally disturbed, as citizens, with what they as experts, and the political leaders they advise, had been unable to accomplish in controlling the nuclear arms race. In less than one hour, they had set aside their antiseptic mode of discourse about arms control, welcomed the symbolic presence of their worried fellow citizens, and started asking themselves and each other "first-order" questions:

• What kind of world are we trying to build, anyhow? It is bound to be a world with nobody in charge; how do we make sure it is a world safe for diversity?

• What is the minimum behavior we need from the Soviets and what is the minimum behavior they need from us, to persuade us mutually not to blow up the world?

• Has the nuclear arms race taken on a life of its own, far beyond rational calculation of anyone's security needs? And if our own security in fact depends on preventing nuclear war, how can we best break out of a mindless spiral while remaining realistic? A military question: Are nuclear weapons really weapons in the sense that they can be used for rationally determined purposes? A political question: Are formal negotiations the only road to arms control and disarmament? What about mutual example and national action, verified not by treaty but by our growing capacity to watch what the other side does?

• Even on the most optimistic assumptions, rethinking our security and arms control policies (and inducing others to do likewise when they perceive we are serious about it) is going to take a while. What do we do until the doctor comes? What can be done to get through the years just ahead, in dealing with conflict and managing the crises we know from experience will keep erupting?

The Humphrey Institute then asked half a dozen specialists to spend part of the summer of 1984 rethinking the rethinkable. They presented their essays at a one-day Minneapolis conference in December 1984, to the citizens who had been involved in the year-long process. The citizens, stimulated by the community dialogue, had a chance to "stump the experts" with their comments and questions. Much rewriting ensued; the resulting essays constitute the chapters that follow.

Another feature of this fifth public forum was a talk by Dean Rusk, former secretary of state; a transcript of his lucid commentary on diplomacy in the nuclear era is reproduced as an afterword to this volume.

In short: what we did in a few months' time was to induce a genuinely fresh look at what embedded U.S. assumptions (the only assumptions Americans can do something about) need rethinking. Any community can do the same. The object is plain and simple: to clear the way for molding future policy based less on hand-me-down premises and always incomplete "facts," and more on a comprehensive view of our *purposes*.

The words captured between the covers of this book are thus the end product of a creative interaction between citizens and specialists. They are, of course, not the end of the needed rethinking. Our hope and belief are that they sketch a new beginning. In the matter of nuclear war, *not* to make a new beginning, and soon, would be the greatest danger of all.

Prospects for Peacemaking

Introduction: The Case for Rethinking
Lincoln P. Bloomfield and Harlan Cleveland

A Moment of Opportunity

For the four decades since 1945, experts and political leaders have been studying, negotiating, and disagreeing about nuclear arms control and disarmament. But now, in the 1980s, something really new has been added: People-in-general, whose eyes glaze over when the experts debate throw-weights and vulnerabilities, elbowed their way to the negotiating tables. Their more active engagement resulted from the dawning of two politically potent ideas.

One of these was that a nuclear winter is possible and could be fatal to the human race even if only one side launched its missiles. The other was a powerful political metaphor called "freeze"—the notion that one obvious way to start stopping the mad momentum of a runaway arms race would be just to stop.

At the beginning of 1984 the two main U.S.-Soviet nuclear arms control negotiations—on strategic weapons ("START") and on intermediate-range nuclear forces in Europe ("INF")—seemed irretrievably hung up. The long-running talks in Vienna on the balance of conventional forces arrayed against each other in Europe ("MBFR") were not only stalled but almost forgotten. The wider Geneva talks on a comprehensive ban on testing nuclear weapons ("CTB") had long been enmeshed in technical disputes that masked a mutual desire to get nowhere. And the talks in Madrid about European security, stemming from the Helsinki Final Act of 1975, had recessed after several years with what amounted to an East-West agreement to disagree.

All this absence of progress reflected a deep mutual distrust between a U.S. president and a collective Soviet leadership who had never even met each other in person.

Then the leaders met. Each was pushed from behind—the American by a gathering public consensus, the Soviet by some indecipherable mix of economic troubles and military worries. A new round of Geneva talks was set in motion. A minisummit in Iceland produced startling "in principle" proposals by both sides ("in principle" means "we haven't really agreed yet but we have to announce *something*"), but was hung up on Soviet fears of, and U.S. hopes for, a space-based antimissile system. Both sides then maneuvered for advantage. For further developments, see your daily newspaper.

If ever there was a moment for hard rethinking, if ever fresh citizen insights and fresh expert analysis were needed to make this new opening real and not another impasse produced by experts on impasses, that moment is now.

Three Paradoxes

How will future historians look back on our own time? What name will they give to the turbulence and kaleidoscopic change we know as the second half of the twentieth century?

If our luck holds, they will not label our epoch the prelude to World War III. But they are quite likely to speak in puzzlement about this age of ideology, of cold war, and of nuclear standoff. And they may also discern a pattern in three grand paradoxes that baffle our own wisepeople.

One is an international system that tripled the number of sovereign states—yet also gave unprecedented powers to such nonstate, boundary-ignoring movers and shakers as IBM, Sony, the Vatican, Shi'a Islam, and, for a time, OPEC.

The second paradox is the widespread enthusiasm for national independence in an uncompromisingly interdependent world—with nobody in charge, despite several self-nominated candidates for world governor.

And the third is knowledge-harnessed-to-technique, including the worldwide spread of information technology that erodes traditional hierarchies and punches great holes in the old protective national bubbles. This dynamic force contrasts with a persistent strength of old-fashioned nationalism, and a steady rate of inter-nation conflicts (about 1.5 a year) featuring such familiar grievances as disputed frontiers, ethnic hatreds, and racial injustice.

Above all, future chroniclers may understand (as many contemporary strategists do not) how radically different from all other weapons nuclear systems are turning out to be, and how irreversible is the fall from political innocence once the fruit of nuclear knowledge is tasted. Even in our own time governments have begun to listen to scientific arguments that a large-scale nuclear war, even an attack with no retaliation, could threaten all human life on the planet. For every sovereign state "national security" contains (whether acknowledged or not) the primary imperative that there must be no nuclear war.

Today's political, educational, and moral leaders thus face a challenge without precedent. But so far, the caution induced by "official" responsibility and the perceived parochialisms of the parishes to which they respond have been more potent motives than the objective need for creativity in inventing security systems for a safer world. It is high time, then, for concerned people—citizens and experts and leaders alike and together—to question the current assumptions about both goals and strategies that have brought us to this watershed in world history.

In this short book we suggest some ways to rethink premises and practices that drive American policymaking. Similar rethinking in other polities and cultures could lay the basis for new kinds of international cooperation. It would be wonderful if the Soviet system permitted a comparable exercise. But our first obligation is to our own rationality.

We have not presumed to seek solutions to all the world's ills. We do not deal in this volume with the economic, social, and religious roots of conflict, important as they are, or with the needed revival of effective multilateral machinery for dispute settlement and cooperation in meeting human needs and guarding human rights.

We *have* focused on the bedrock issues of nuclear peace: U.S.-Soviet relations, the military use of nuclear explosions, nuclear arms control policy, and nuclear crisis management. "Peace" cannot mean no turbulence, no disputes, no organized violence. The minimal definition of "peace" is a condition in which the chances of a nuclear war are reduced to near zero, while the unending effort continues to cope with conflicts in the human family.

The Trust Factor

The essential linkage of arms control to national security used to be taken as axiomatic. Since the middle 1970s that linkage has been thrown into question by critics of the several arms control treaties negotiated with the Soviet Union by Presidents Nixon, Ford, and Carter.

Experts and politicians in the United States (and doubtless in the Soviet Union too) turned out to be divided between two very different concepts of the proper path to improved security. In the 1960s and half of the 1970s the prevalent opinion (still agreed to by consistent majorities of citizens) favored arms control for its own sake. Almost any agreement on limiting nuclear arms, virtually regardless of its details, indeed even negotiation itself, seemed a good thing.

The reason also seemed self-evident: regardless of U.S.-Soviet political differences—and they are many—the nuclear arms competition is too dangerous, expensive, and irrational to permit it to be held hostage to Afghanistan, human rights abuses, and other legitimate complaints about Soviet behavior. In this view the superpowers face not only each other but an even more threatening common enemy: nuclear weaponry. The game that must be played between them thus is not and cannot be "zero-sum" in which all is competitive and one's loss is always the other's gain. It is, rather, a "cooperative-sum" game in which both either "win" or lose together.

A contrary view has always existed, deeply and more comprehensively skeptical of any agreement with the Soviets. Opposition to the dominant arms control consensus was galvanized by ratification in 1972 of the SALT I treaty limiting antiballistic missile defenses, and the 1979 signing of SALT II putting a cap on strategic delivery systems. In 1981 a U.S. president who shared these doubts and had campaigned against these treaties took office. At root, the antiarms control position interpreted the struggle between the Soviet and American systems as zero-sum, and destined to be fought out at every level. In this perspective, arms control seemed to ratify Soviet superiority, negotiation could only be delusion, and strategic superiority was not only crucial to victory but actually attainable.

This attitude institutionalizes mistrust. It is curiously parallel to the thinking of hard-line Marxist-Leninists on the other side; both insist on the permanent and unremitting nature of the clash between systems. Carried to its logical extreme, this attitude makes genuine arms control depend on major changes not in the opponent's negotiating policy, but at the very roots of its domestic system.

Without rehearsing here the lugubrious history of the collapse of the detente of the 1970s, we can acknowledge as factual the self-defeating Soviet policy of exploiting—in such neuralgic spots as Angola, Yemen, Ethiopia, and above all Afghanistan—the retreat of American power and political will, in the wake of Vietnam. In this sense Americans could legitimately believe that an important part of the U.S. agenda for detente—mutual self-restraint in turbulent Third World areas—had been betrayed. We can also leave it to the historians to judge the extent to which the United States reneged on Moscow's cherished agenda item of greatly expanded trade and access to modern technology.

As a matter of historic fact, even the most ardent advocates of arms control within both capitals have always had to place it within the context of overall strategy, as a kind of strategic subset that mades the competition safer, more predictable, and less costly. As of the late 1980s the two sides have once again recognized the high desirability of agreed limits to what is emerging as a far more expensive and destabilizing phase of the nuclear competition. It is more important than ever for the citizens in a democratic country to understand what is happening and to make informed judgments that their leaders must respect.

The Rules Have Changed

In considering the chapters that follow, the reader should be aware of several crucial changes, some of them still over the horizon, in the nature of the security problem.

One change is in the very things with which strategic arms agreements deal. The two SALT agreements placed limitations on the vehicles that carry weapons—the so-called launchers. Even during the recent hard times for agreements there has been a growing acknowledgment on both sides of the need for a more realistic and complex kind of unit of measurement.

The United States and the U.S.S.R. have quite different problems of national security based on their very different geography, neighbors, and traditions. It is increasingly hard to differentiate between strategic and tactical weapons, or those called theater, or United States versus allied, and so forth. A package of weaponry for each may be quite a different mix that takes into account real-world variety, as well as "counting rules" based on comparable units of account such as warheads and yield.

Another possible change is in the process. The conventional wisdom still looks for formal negotiated agreements. But some have long proposed unilateral measures of restraint as bait, so to speak, for reciprocated measures on the other side. U.S. Arms Control Agency Director Kenneth Adelman has argued publicly for bypassing the treaty process his colleagues seemed to fear—while in fact taking parallel stabilizing measures and even making numerical cuts, which presumably could be later negotiated.

Ronald Reagan's advocacy since 1983 of what some deem a highly questionable space-based missile defense underscored the fact that in an important sense the race is not between the two superpowers so much as it is between their control over policy and the inexorable momentum of their own technologies. New and troubling questions are raised about their ability to ride out future crises without intolerable pressures to preempt, given the fantastic "improvements" in microminiaturized hardware such as missile guidance systems and the software for high-speed electronic dataprocessing. In recognition of this crucial trend, the Scowcroft Commission appointed by President Reagan urged moving toward more "crisis-stable" systems such as mobile single-warhead missiles.

A whole new element was introduced into an already complex equation with what the Reagan administration christened its Strategic Defense Initiative ("SDI") and others labeled "Star Wars." Defense is morally attractive compared with threats of mutual annihilation—always assuming we can get to the end of the development process without introducing potentially catastrophic instability into the inevitable crises along the way.

Sometimes unnoticed in the concentration on nuclear weaponry are the enormous changes wrought in "conventional" weaponry by the same technological dynamic. (The great bulk of the world's $1 trillion of annual arms expenditures goes for conventional weapons, many of them used in so-called small wars, which many believe could be the trigger for any big war.) The manned bomber has acquired a new lease on life with accurate standoff cruise missiles and so-called Stealth technology. Submarines today provide the most survivable deterrent of all, but in time the race for effective antisubmarine techniques could make the oceans dangerously transparent.

The benign face of technology supplies an increasing capacity to verify what the other side is doing, through remote sensing, superior cameras and radars, and improved instrumentation. More startling and probably less benign is the way new technology blurs the threshold between nuclear and non-nuclear weaponry with dual-capable systems and munitions that can fight strategic-type battles. Parallel developments in electronics, software, sensors, and materials make possible precision navigation and automated battle management that requires rapid collection and dissemination of target information.

All this does not change the crucial difference in the nature of nuclear explosives. The point is that the qualitative technology race is changing the rules that have dominated deterrence strategy, potentially jeopardizing the crisis stability that, at the end of the day, is the only real payoff for this whole security effort. The only long-term strategy that will rationally protect the national security is one that protects not just ours but others' as well. The only self-interested national security policy is one that aims at constantly raising the nuclear threshold, while making certain that the accelerating move toward "smart" conventional weaponry does not have the perverse effect of making big wars thinkable again.

Where We Could Be

U.S. national security policies cross some unstable fault lines, and deep stirrings are felt below. The antinuclear popular movements that came (and in some cases went) in the early 1980s could be discounted as emotional reactions to unacceptably casual pronouncements about nuclear war. But they also reflected a troubling public fatalism, confirmed in poll after poll, that saw nuclear war as increasingly likely. In the same period the normally cautious Conference of U.S. Catholic Bishops questioned the morality of nuclear deterrence, the very centerpiece of current U.S. defense policy. And President Reagan's call for a crash research effort to develop a space-based defense system spoke to the frustration of many Americans

with an overhanging Damoclean sword that threatens us all
with annihilation—sometime.

Neither the bishops nor the president furnished currently
workable prescriptions for the diseases they correctly diag-
nosed. Struggling with the morality of deterrence, the bishops
acknowledged that the greater sin would be to fail to prevent
nuclear adventurism. And perversely, the likeliest candidate to
weaken deterrence could be a one-sided lead in missile defenses. Yet the deep contradictions in the contemporary "security system" will have to be faced, and soon.

At the heart of the nuclear security problem lies the competitive relationship between the United States and the Soviet
Union, charter members of that exclusive club with the capacity
to terminate life on earth as a means of settling disputes. It is
no Cold War obsession to note that Soviet leadership, from one
decade to another, operates on a set of premises and operating
rules that profoundly clash with those of the world's political
democracies. U.S. and Soviet leaders are at one in asserting that
their competitive coexistence must not end in war. Yet the
forty-year postwar relationship between the nuclear giants re-
sembles a chronic fever chart. Neither leadership has found it
possible to break fresh ground beyond the well-worn path they
have warily trod.

In his essay Marshall Shulman, the veteran expert on the
U.S.S.R. and former U.S. ambassador-at-large who headed Columbia University's Harriman Institute for the Advanced Study
of the Soviet Union, tackles the questions Minnesota citizens
put to him: What kind of altered relationship would make possible the pursuit of the vital interests of both great nations?
What minimum behavior on the part of each is required? And
what policies, parallel actions, self-constraints, and reasonable
risks would such a bargain entail?

Professional strategists have been slower than other citizens
to grasp the massive differences in scale and consequence between nuclear and nonnuclear war. Retired U.S. Vice Admiral
John Marshall Lee, providing chapter and verse, reviews the
military categories against which that difference must be
professionally tested: deterrence, war-fighting, political influence, and accidental use. The professional inclination to think
of genocidal explosions as "weapons" may, he suggests, be central to the problems we face.

Given the meager results of four decades of sporadic negotiations, arms control diplomacy has been patently inadequate to its assigned task. The ruts are deep, the engine in low gear when it runs at all, the chief actors jerky and arthritic in their movements. The diplomatic process has shifted around among the superpowers, the alliances, the United Nations, and groups in between. Whatever the venue, instructions to negotiators faithfully mirror each government's fears, its internal disagreements, its analytical skills, and its perception of the intentions of others. But the problem is not the processes; it is the lack of outcomes while military technology races ahead of treaty making. In the short run, agreements to talk are good politics, inside countries and among them. In the longer run, talks without agreement can become in themselves a danger to peace.

Michael Nacht of the University of Maryland and Jane Sharp of London's Royal Institute of International Affairs (formerly of Cornell University) are two political scientists known for their imaginative—and differing—approaches to arms control. Each was asked how we get out of the rut we are in: whether negotiations can ever keep up with technology; how to judge qualitative as well as quantitative arms control measures; what nourishment there may be in nonnegotiated mutual example and reciprocal national actions; whether "no first use" of nuclear weapons can be married to a viable conventional defense in Europe; how to think about the puzzles of "verification"; and how, in every nation, domestic politics constrains the diplomacy of arms reduction.

Even if a new start can be made toward turning back the nuclear juggernaut, it is supremely important that the strategic balance remain stable during the inevitable crises that periodically send decision makers to their command posts in Washington and Moscow. Given effective nuclear deterrence, a "bolt from the blue" surprise attack remains the least likely eventuality. But both superpowers are pushed and pulled by allies and clients into dangerous juxtaposition on opposing sides of "local" conflicts. In a world of probable nuclear spread and nuclear terrorism, whether by impulsive states or reckless nongovernments, each superpower will from time to time go on precautionary alerts that will, in turn, send a potentially menacing signal to the other.

Lincoln P. Bloomfield of the Massachusetts Institute of Technology, drawing on his experience in the State Department and the National Security Council, explores "what to do until the doctor comes." He reviews developments in weapons and strategies that make for crisis instability, and then assesses command, control, and communications in the light of well-documented malfunctions and impairments—not only of machines but of individuals and groups under conditions of stress, uncertainty, and information overload. What goes on in the world's emergency rooms is evidently in urgent need of rethinking, too.

1

A Citizen's Approach to Soviet-American Relations
Marshall Shulman

Citizens who are concerned about the danger of nuclear war find it hard to understand why the United States and the Soviet Union are locked into a conflicted relationship.

They ask, Why are the two countries at swords' points with each other? What are the root causes of the tension between them? Why, even if there are serious differences between the two countries, can they not agree to reduce the danger of nuclear war when it is so obviously in the interests of both countries to do so?

Why is it not possible to have a dialogue between the two leaders along the following lines?

An Imaginary Dialogue

Suppose for a moment that the leaders of the Soviet Union and the United States were to meet at some future time, and were able to talk to each other like this:

American president: The present situation is insane. Both your country and mine are pouring vast resources into building weapons of destruction. Not only is it costly, and preventing us from using these resources in more constructive ways, but it is dangerous. Each day we move, both of us, toward weapons that are more destructive, and we are both on edge against the possibility of being attacked, and destroyed. Given the fallibility of human beings and of the weapons, the computers that control them, the sources of our information from radar and satellites, and the very brief time we would each have to make crucial decisions, this is a precarious situation to be in. This is not in the interest of your country or of mine. Can't we back away from this dangerous situation?

Soviet leader: I agree with what you say. It makes no sense at all. But as we see it, your country is mainly responsible for this situation. You have taken the lead in developing new weapons. You have an

economy twice the size of ours, and a much more powerful base in
new technology. So long as you keep building new weapons, we have
to keep up with you.

American president: But as we see it, your country threatens us.
We cannot see that your legitimate defense needs justify so many
powerful weapons. We are uneasy about your intentions. Your whole
way of thinking, your ideology, is rooted in the notion that your system and ours are historically hostile to each other, and that yours will
someday emerge as dominant.

Soviet leader: It is true that our systems are different, and that we
believe yours has inner contradictions that will cause its collapse. We
also fear that you will use force to try to prevent that from happening.
We see your government as trying to undermine our system, and to
overpower us. But we believe that the differences between our two
systems can be left to the judgment of history, and should not be
settled in war.

American president: Let us agree that the two systems are different, and that the two countries have different values and different
interests. You say that you are prepared to leave this to the judgment
of history, but it doesn't appear to us that this is what you are doing.
Everywhere, we are in competition. You arm and encourage revolutionary movements . . .

Soviet leader: Your country sends more arms abroad than we do.
You have military bases abroad, some of them quite close to us. Don't
we have reasons to worry about your intentions?

American president: But even if we aren't able to resolve the competitive relationship between our two countries, could we not at least
agree that a nuclear war would be a disaster for all of us, no matter
how it started?

Soviet leader: Of course that is so, and it worries us. But you are
ahead of us in many kinds of new nuclear weapons, and you keep
planning new ones. We will not disarm while you are arming.

American president: We think your country is ahead in some important respects, and we are trying to protect ourselves against any
eventualities. But since neither of us can hope to have enough nuclear weapons to attack the other without being destroyed, why can't
we reverse this trend, and move toward an equal balance at lower
levels?

Soviet leader: It would make sense. We have often proposed it,
even the total elimination of all nuclear weapons.

American president: It is too hard to see how we could do that, but
let's not let the best be the enemy of the good. Suppose we were each
to reduce our total nuclear weapons by some small amount the first
year, and more the second year, and so on, until we were down to
lower levels. At least we would reverse the trend.

Soviet leader: It would make good sense. But we would worry that
your country has the possibilities in reserve to spring new systems on
us in a short time.

American president: Well, frankly we don't trust your country either. We would each have to verify that the other was making the promised reductions. Can you accept that?

Soviet leader: We have always feared that your demands for on-site inspection would be an excuse for intrusive espionage. But we could probably manage to allow inspection of the reductions.

American president: Since the reductions would be small, neither country would be defenseless, and even if we got down to half of our present levels, we would still have more than enough to destroy each other in retaliation against attack. But if we were both moving downward, there would be less incentive to be developing new weapons.

Soviet leader: If we were both moving downward, we would reach a point at which it would be necessary to bring China and France and Britain into the picture.

American president: Indeed we shall have to try to do that, and also to cooperate to reduce the spread of nuclear weapons to other countries.

Soviet leader: That is correct. Let us begin with these small reductions. There would still be many dangers of conflicts; the world would still not be safe, but it would be better.

American president: Yes, perhaps in time as we developed confidence, we could then do something about conventional weapons too. We are worried about your large armies. Even a conventional war could be very destructive.

Soviet leader: That could be a next step. And we would hope that you would also be willing to move toward better trade relations, and toward consulting with us on the Middle East and other regional problems.

American president: That might become possible. But our first priority is to reduce the danger of nuclear war.

What Are the Obstacles?

Such a dialogue seems farfetched under present circumstances. Why is this so? Can we understand better what are the obstacles, on the American side and on the Soviet side, to a move in this direction? And what can be done about these obstacles?

The American Side
Popular hostility toward the Soviet Union goes back to the Soviet Revolution in 1917. The revolutionary ideology of Marxism-Leninism, with its expressed aspirations for the worldwide triumph of Communism, aroused deep suspicions and apprehensions. The fear of Communism became a profound motif in American political life, and a point of orientation for American foreign policy. Episodes of attempts at subversion and espionage, Soviet support for revolutionary activity in the world,

and hostile Soviet propaganda predicting the collapse of capitalism, all contributed to these apprehensions.

For most of the seven decades since the Soviet Revolution, relations between the two countries have been bad, with only a few periods of reduced tension and hope for improvement. One such period came in 1934, at the time diplomatic relations was established between the two countries. But the Soviet pledges of noninterference in the domestic life of other countries were not honored. Another such period came during World War II, when the two countries were linked in the "Grand Alliance." But cooperation during the war was limited by Stalin's suspicions, and as the war ended, the Soviet Union began taking over control of Eastern Europe, in violation of its commitment under the Yalta agreement to guarantee representative governments in these countries. Disillusionment about the expectations that our "gallant Allies" would be partners in the postwar settlements intensified the hostility during the Cold War that followed.

During the brief so-called "détente" period, which had its high point during the 1972 visit of President Nixon to Moscow and the signing of the first SALT treaty and other agreements, there were again expectations of a lasting improvement in the relationship, but the two countries had different understandings of what a "détente" relationship meant. Soviet actions in Angola and Ethiopia, exploiting these local conflict situations to extend their influence in Africa, appeared to Americans as a violation of the restraints they expected of the "détente" relationship. The Soviet invasion of Afghanistan in 1979, although by that time not much was left of the "détente," was a final blow to remaining expectations of improved relations. The Soviet military buildup since 1963 enabled the Soviet Union to achieve strategic parity with the United States by about 1970, but it appeared to the United States that the buildup was continued more than could be justified by any defensive purposes. Soviet violations of basic human rights in the treatment of domestic opposition, Soviet impediments to free emigration from the country, and its antireligious policies contributed to strong popular antipathy toward the Soviet Union.

Problems within the United States intensified this antipathy. The aftereffects of the U.S. defeat in Vietnam, and the resulting reaction against interventionist policies, deepened the sense of impotence many Americans felt in the face of Soviet actions in Angola and Ethiopia. So did the hostage situation in Iran, although this was not related to any action by the Soviet Union. These events and more contributed to a hardening of American attitudes toward the Soviet Union, expressed in the election campaign of 1980.

These developments coincided with a conservative swing in American politics, which, although mainly directed at domestic sentiment resentful of the growth of the federal government, combined with a resurgence of nationalism to harden further attitudes toward the Soviet Union, and to discredit any moves toward improved relations with the Soviet Union as appeasement.

Because the United States for most of its history has been an insular country and its people have relatively little knowledge of other political cultures, discussion of foreign policy problems, including relations with the Soviet Union, tends to be conducted in oversimplified terms. Policy alternatives are cast into polarized stereotypes, between "hard" and "soft," between Cold War and détente, based upon cartoon images of the Soviet Union and its political life. Little of the knowledge developed by scholars about the complexities of Soviet society have entered into public discussion, or into decision making by the government.

The process by which decisions are made on foreign policy in the United States has also made it more difficult to have a balanced and coherent policy toward the Soviet Union. As a reaction to years in which presidents tended to act on their own in the determination of foreign policy, particularly during the Vietnam War, Congress has become more assertive in this field, but the weakening of the authority of the leadership of Congress and of its committee chairmen has further limited the capability of the government for concerted decision making.

Also, in decision making regarding defense policy, the process has worked against rational decisions in the national interest. Parochial interests have been stronger than any expression of the overall national interest. The individual military services, the economic interests of the weapons industry, and their supporters in Congress concerned about military jobs in their areas have had more influence in decisions about new weapons systems than any overarching articulation of the national interest.

Starting from traditional American attitudes toward military policy, which go back to reliance on the "six-shooter" at one's hip as the best form of security on the frontier, the disposition of the country has been to believe that security is best assured by having superiority over any adversary. This belief has been slow to take account of the way nuclear weapons and missiles affect international security. The public constituency in support of arms control has been relatively weak, and there has not been strong presidential leadership to strengthen this constituency. This was demonstrated in the failure of the United States to ratify the SALT II treaty. Although there is widespread concern about the danger of nuclear war, this sentiment has not been strong enough or constant enough to be a politically effective force in this country—and it is inhibited by prevalent mistrust of the Soviet Union.

These are some of the obstacles that would have to be overcome before a president of the United States, even if he were so inclined, could feel that he had sufficient popular support to take the kind of initiative described in our imaginary dialogue.

The Soviet Side

What about the obstacles on the Soviet side? The first and most obvious problem is that the Soviet system has not, until now, been able to solve a prolonged succession problem. It has not been able to produce a strong and vigorous central leadership, and the direction of the country has been in the hands of a group of men, most of whom are in their 70s, set in their ways, limited in their perspectives, capable of reacting to events but not capable of decisive initiatives either in domestic or in foreign policy.

Sooner or later, it was inevitable that a younger generation would come to power, but we still cannot predict with confidence that Gorbachev will necessarily be more pragmatic and flexible than the older leaders have been.

The Soviet system has many serious problems, the most pressing of which is the state of the economy. The Soviet economy has been growing, but at a slower and slower rate in recent years, reflecting low productivity in both agriculture and industry. The extreme centralization of the Soviet political system creates bottlenecks and inhibits innovation, and the Soviet Union has been lagging behind other industrial societies in the development of advanced technology. There is active discussion of the reforms that are needed, but the vast bureaucracy resists change. Many party officials fear that economic reforms may weaken the authority of the party. Labor morale is low and there is widespread corruption and drunkenness. The population is by and large conservative in its resistance to change.

There are other problems. One is the increasing population ratio of the minority nationalities and their pressure for self-expression; the Russian population is becoming a minority in the Soviet Union.

There is widespread dissatisfaction, particularly over economic shortages, but there is no evidence that this approaches revolutionary intensity. In any case, the political police—the KGB—is large and strong and is capable of controlling any expression of opposition to the regime.

Contrary to the widespread impression in the United States that the Soviet Union has been successfully on the march in the world, prospects for Soviet foreign policy are not promising. In Eastern Europe, the Soviet Union faces restiveness in varying degrees, most acutely in Poland, but also in some degree in Hungary, East Germany, Rumania, and even Bulgaria. It has been a drain on Soviet resources to try to prevent economic shortages in Eastern Europe from triggering political and nationalist manifestations. The Soviet Union has not been able to work out its differences with China, and it fears the day when the Chinese will have a large arsenal of nuclear weapons. The Soviet Union has not been able to turn to advantage strains between the United States and Japan or Western Europe, and its influence in the Middle East and in Southern Africa has diminished. Nowhere in the world today do people find inspiration in the Soviet ideology or the Soviet example as a model to follow.

Within the Soviet Union, the Marxist-Leninist ideology has also lost much of its force. Most younger people regard it with cynicism, and are more interested in materialistic personal goals. Some of the ideas of Marxism-Leninism—such as the belief that capitalism is doomed to decay—still have wide acceptance, but for the most part, Soviet actions in the world are determined by its nation-state interests, although ideological language is often used to rationalize these actions after the fact, and ideological slogans and rhetoric are advanced on national holidays.

In historical perspective, the Soviet Union has been going through a period of virile national growth, like that which other European nations experienced in earlier centuries. It has emerged on the world stage as a superpower, largely by virtue of its great military power and its progress in outer space—and the fact that other European countries were also weakened in two world wars. The Soviet Union seeks for itself recognition as a superpower of equal status with the United States, and it smarts under the indications that its internal weaknesses prevent it from receiving that recognition. It is determined, however, not to be seen as weak, and it reacts strongly to any challenge to its status.

By putting more than an eighth of its annual product into the military sector, the Soviet Union has achieved parity in strategic weapons with the United States, but it now faces serious decisions about whether to increase this military expenditure to match the continuing military buildup of the United States. It can do so, but at the cost of a still further postponement of any hope of building a modern industrial technology, and a further tightening of standards of living. These costs provide an incentive for the Soviet Union to seek serious arms control negotiations with the United States, but Soviet leaders still are not sure the United States is prepared to negotiate seriously.

The Soviets currently perceive the United States as threatening. They see the United States as having enormous military power and the economic and technological capability to increase it still further. They see the worldwide alliances of the United States, with its weapons deployed abroad in many foreign bases, as a source of intimidating pressure, if not worse, and they feel that the United States is currently seeking to undermine the Soviet regime.

On the Soviet side, these are some of the obstacles to a dialogue with the United States such as we have described.

How to Reduce the Danger of Nuclear War?

During the past thirty years each side has, from time to time, groped toward some improvement in relations with the other. These efforts were generally mounted against domestic opposition, and were not fully developed or consistently applied.

Moreover, with the exception of the 1972 period, the moods of the two countries were not synchronous. While one side was prepared at least to explore the possibilities for some improvement in the relationship, the other was still reacting to earlier challenges and was slow to perceive or accept the possibilities of change when they appeared. In each case, the depth of the resistance to such efforts and their qualified and equivocal character only illustrate the profound obstacles that have to be overcome to change the relationship sufficiently to reduce the danger of war.

Nevertheless, it is a useful exercise to try to clarify our thinking about what minimum changes in behavior would be needed from each side to make possible a more rational management of the nuclear military competition, even while other aspects of their competitive relationship might continue, as it seems probable they will do for some time.

Changes on the Soviet Side

The first, most obvious, and most important change would have to be a greater exercise of restraint in *military matters*. The Soviet Union would need to be willing to accept a balance of mutual deterrence at lower levels. This would relieve pressures on Soviet economic resources, and might have support from those who maintain that the strengthening of the base of industrial technology is more important than additions to the arsenal. This would mean restraint in the production of new weapons and in the deployment of existing weapons, ranging from intercontinental to short range.

Greater Soviet cooperation would be required in providing for better methods of verification. This would require acceptance by the Soviet Union of some forms of inspection, in ways that would not be so intrusive as to compromise its legitimate security interests. Some move in this direction was made by the Soviet Union during the negotiations on a comprehensive test ban, when it indicated a willingness to accept on its territory "black boxes" containing seismic recorders. Some limitations would also be desirable in its encryption of telemetry from missile tests, so that the United States could be assured of their nonthreatening character.

Many of these steps would be achieved if the Soviet Union and the United States were able to complete negotiations on a comprehensive test ban and on central strategic weapons and theater nuclear weapons. But even in the absence of such agreements, the steps could be taken unilaterally if they were reciprocated by the other side.

Either way, these steps would require an assertion of political control over military decision making, reversing the recent trend toward a greater degree of autonomy for the Soviet military in the face of the weaker leadership of the Communist Party. These measures therefore presuppose that Gorbachev will have had time to consolidate his authority.

When it comes to *political competition* in the Third World, other measures of restraint would be necessary. It may be that the Soviet Union will have learned from the experience of other imperial countries, and from its own experience, that empires are costly and that foreign colonies do not yield the advantages they may appear to offer. Whatever validity Soviet leaders may have attached to Lenin's theory of imperialism (that the acquisition of colonies stems from the desire for foreign markets and sources of raw materials), modern Soviet leaders may come to recognize that under present conditions of international politics, it is not necessary or even advantageous to acquire political control over foreign countries in order to have access to their markets or their raw materials.

Moreover, the lessons of recent years suggest that military intervention to produce or prevent political change does not lead to productive relations, and cannot substitute for local political support. The United States learned this lesson in Vietnam, and the Soviet Union is currently finding this to be true in Afghanistan.

Doubtless the political competition will continue, but if the risk of escalation from local conflict situations is to be reduced, it will be necessary to work toward at least tacit limits on the levels and means of intervention by the Soviet Union, and by the United States as well, in those conflicts. Efforts in the past to work out codes of conduct across the board have not been successful, since local conditions and the relative intensity of interest of the two sides vary from one area to another, but on a region-by-region basis it should be possible to agree, tacitly if not explicitly, on what levels of weapons and personnel could be accepted by the two sides, within the reasonable bounds of competition, without leading to a dangerous escalation of the conflict.

Since Soviet intervention in Third World conflicts has been justified by reference to the ideological theme of support for National Liberation Movements, this leads to the more fundamental question of how far modifications in the Soviet *ideology* would be required to reduce the danger of war. It seems evident that, whether in its formal ideological declarations or at least in its tacit operating beliefs, it would be necessary for the Soviet Union to put behind it the commitment to the idea of conflict in some form between differing social systems.

The Soviet Union has clearly moved a long distance from its early commitment to autarky to a substantial involvement in the world economic system. Under Gorbachev there has begun to be acknowledgment that in this interdependent world, the Soviet economy and its fate are inevitably and inextricably bound up with the global economy, and cannot be separated from the concerns of other nations regarding the global environment.

Perhaps the most far-reaching step, and one that may take longer than any other, would be the acceptance by the Soviet Union of its own self-interest in strengthening the *international system*, which it has tended to regard as hostile to its interests. This does not mean accepting the status quo, but it does mean accepting the principle of peaceful change and the avoidance of force in trying to produce or prevent political change. In the long run, it would be necessary for the Soviet Union to come to the recognition that its own security cannot be separated from, or be in opposition to, the international system—that is, to an acceptance of the restraints on national sovereignty required to strengthen the codification of the accepted behavior of nations in the world against the chaos and violence of international anarchy.

There is one final point that needs to be considered. Some writers argue that certain *internal changes* within the Soviet Union are necessary, in the direction of an observance of human rights and the democratization of the society, if war is to be avoided. Changes in this direction are obviously desirable, but the question is whether they are a necessary condition for peaceful relations. The argument that they are necessary rests upon the proposition that Soviet aggressiveness is inherently rooted in the nature of its system, and that its behavior abroad cannot be modified unless the system is fundamentally changed. But in fact Soviet behavior in the world has been much modified over the past thirty years, in response to the external environment. The lesson of this experience should be that such changes can best be induced by a combination of constraints and incentives. If we were to take as our objective the imposition of fundamental changes in the Soviet system, the result would surely be a mobilization of the Soviet Union and a heightening of its repressive practices, to confront a hostile environment. On the other hand, an environment that is resistant to Soviet expansionism but is nonthreatening and encourages cooperative behavior is more likely to allow forces for change from within to modify repressive practices.

Changes on the United States Side

From the Soviet point of view, the most important requirement of the United States in the *military* sphere is that it should accept the principles of parity and equal security. By this, the Soviets mean that any arms control agreements should not give the United States superiority, or result in any relative disadvantage to the Soviet Union. But they also have in mind that the U.S.S.R. needs a larger military force than does the United States, to deal with other possible adversaries, including China, France, and the United Kingdom, and also to compensate for the possible unreliability of their East European allies.

This argument does not require larger nuclear forces for the Soviet Union than for the United States, if both sides accept the principle of mutual deterrence, since a gross parity of strategic nuclear weapons would serve to deter each of the Soviet Union's possible adversaries, alone or in combination. The Soviet Union's legitimate security needs would be met if the United States were to make clear in its actions, as well as its declaratory policy, that it does not seek to achieve military superiority over the Soviet Union, and that it recognizes that any agreements should not seek to alter the military balance to the disadvantage of the Soviet Union.

The United States would need genuinely to accept the proposition that its security is best protected by a military balance of stable weapons systems at levels as moderate as can be negotiated. This implies an acceptance of mutual deterrence as defining our strategic military requirements, rather than a nuclear war-fighting capability. It also implies that the United States should opt for stable weapons systems (that is, systems that are relatively invulnerable and do not have to be fired quickly lest they be destroyed), thus making it clear that it is not seeking to acquire the capacity to strike first.

Commitments along these lines would mean not only restraint in the production of new weapons systems, but avoiding systems that are destabilizing, such as the powerful MX land-based missile or the so-called "Strategic Defense Initiative," which would involve antisatellite and antiballistic missile systems based in space. Nor would the United States deploy systems that are difficult to verify, such as the sea-launched cruise missiles that it has now begun to deploy.

As in the case of the Soviet Union, these measures would follow automatically if agreement were reached on a comprehensive test ban, on central strategic weapons and theater nuclear weapons, and if the United States would not undermine or abrogate the antiballistic missile treaty. But even if it were not possible to complete negotiations on those treaties, the measures could be taken unilaterally, subject to reciprocal action on the part of the Soviet Union.

From our review of the obstacles in the United States to movement in these directions, it is evident that such movement would only be possible if there were strong presidential leadership committed to arms control as a central element of our security policy.

With regard to the *political competition* in the Third World, the first requirement for the United States would be that it recognize the local factors involved in Third World upheavals, and not regard the Soviet Union as responsible for all such eruptions. This implies that the United States would not treat all such local conflicts primarily as East-West confrontations, but would seek to deal with the sources of unrest and protest movements with appropriate and constructive attention to local economic and political conditions.

Further, the United States would have to accept for itself, as it would ask of the Soviet Union, restraint against intervention by force to produce or prevent political change in the Third World. The United States would not need to regard as objectionable every increase of Soviet influence, providing that the Soviet Union not threaten areas of vital interest to the United States or that Soviet strength not be of such a magnitude as to threaten the independence of other countries. In other words, "containment" would not be interpreted to mean that the Soviet Union should be prevented from peaceful expansion of its economic or political relations in nonthreatening ways.

It would also follow that the United States would be prepared to observe the tacit or explicitly agreed-on limits on levels and means of intervention in conflicted areas as worked out on a region-by-region basis with the Soviet Union, with the aim of reducing the risk of escalation.

Although our present exercise does not seek the millennial

goal of transforming the Soviet-American relationship altogether, but is limited to the question of what minimum changes of behavior would be necessary to reduce the danger of war, it cannot leave aside the context of their *political relationship*. It has been evident that measures to moderate the military competition are in practice difficult when political tensions are high, although in logic they are more needed at such times. From the Soviet point of view, the minimum condition that would be required to make possible the kind of changes here discussed would be that America not be committed to a confrontationist policy, or to the objective of seeking to undermine the Soviet system.

Finally, if it is the purpose of the United States to persuade the Soviet Union that its self-interest requires acceptance of and support for the *international system*, the United States would need to recognize more clearly than it has done that the strengthening of the international system is also of cardinal importance to U.S. security and interests. This means that we should not be tempted, in our competition with the Soviet Union, to violate international law or to flout the authority of such international institutions as the World Court.

Conclusion

Are these measures unrealistic?

It is true they would require substantial changes from present attitudes both in the United States and the Soviet Union. But nothing less than these is likely to reverse the present trends that are leading toward confrontation and the danger of war. Compared with the alternative, the steps proposed cannot be regarded as unrealistic.

There are limits on how far the United States can influence Soviet behavior. If the Soviet Union shows a lack of restraint in its military and foreign policies, the United States will have no choice but to protect its interests, firmly but with reasonable proportionality. But it should never cease to make clear that when and if present or future leaders of the Soviet Union see their self-interest in policies of restraint and responsibility, the United States is also prepared through its own restraint and responsibility to accept a less dangerous and more productive relationship.

2

The Use and Nonuse of Nuclear Weapons
John Marshall Lee

To deal with the possibility of catastrophic nuclear war between the United States and the U.S.S.R., there are in the military field three general policies to choose among. These are: a war-winning policy, necessarily anchored on a near-perfect defense; a war-controlling (or war-fighting or countervailing) policy, designed to deter nuclear or conventional aggression or, that failing, to fight it without escalating to catastrophe; and a policy of minimizing the nuclear role, restricting the task of nuclear weapons to deterring nuclear, and only nuclear, attack.

The conclusions herein are:

• The war-winning policy is technologically impractical, dangerously destabilizing, and a powerful stimulant to open-ended arms competition. It should not be adopted.

• The war-controlling policy is critically defective in that, first, successful limitation and control of nuclear war is highly improbable, and, second, successful extended deterrence of all types of U.S.-U.S.S.R. hostilities, for the indefinite future, where a single failure would mean disaster, cannot be counted on.

• The minimizing policy, restricting the nuclear role to nuclear deterrence alone, based on such implementing policies as No-First-Use, No-Firing-On-Warning, and No Immediate-Response, with the nuclear and conventional forces tailored to the role, has promise of preventing nuclear weapon use even during U.S.-U.S.S.R. hostilities. It is the recommended path.

It is likewise the recommended policy for other nuclear powers.

The Nuclear Boundary

The nuclear weapon exists. It is unlikely, highly unlikely, that it can be eliminated; the world will have to live with it. A key question is, what use is this appalling device? What can it really accomplish, either actually fired or as a deterrent?

In reaching for answers, the central nuclear relationship to examine is at present that between the Soviet Union and the United States. Theirs are the weapons capable of apocalyptic destruction of each other and many others, conceivably of ending human life.

The Soviet Union, with its powerful, numerically superior conventional forces, enormous geographical expanse, and central strategic position, is nearly invulnerable to conventional attack; the United States and its allies cannot seriously contemplate invading and subduing the U.S.S.R. Thus, as long as any hostilities that may occur remain nonnuclear, the Soviet homeland is fundamentally secure. If the nuclear barrier were breached, however, and a general nuclear war against cities, industry, and the fabric of the countries were to follow, the U.S.S.R. and its allies would almost certainly be destroyed as functioning societies. The United States, behind its oceans, is in a similar position: secure from conventional attack, entirely vulnerable to nuclear weapons. In the literal sense of "vital," the sole truly vital interest of both countries is to prevent general nuclear war between them.

This shared vital interest is the ultimate reality of the nuclear age. Each side is finally dependent upon the other for literal survival. Neither can protect itself from unimaginable destruction if the other launches its nuclear forces against the cities. Even the side that is losing a war can destroy the other. Neither can force the other into final submission. At the heart of the matter, the relationship, strangely but necessarily, is one of cooperation. If the two nations are to survive, there must finally be nuclear cooperation even during active hostilities.

Both sides understand their need to prevent general nuclear war. It weighs continually upon leaders and decision makers, massively in periods of tension. A governmental order to launch nuclear weapons, on any scale, would be a staggering decision. It would be recognized as such. It would be a terrible moment. The probability of it occuring is, at any moment, slight. Still, it is not zero; the risk persists.

Much of that risk follows from applying prenuclear thinking to the nuclear problem, from treating nuclear weapons as merely immensely more powerful versions of conventional weapons, usable, ultimately, as conventional weapons are, for achieving national purposes. Since Nagasaki, the United States has considered using nuclear weapons, more or less seriously, some twenty times, from Iran to Korea to Dien Bien Phu to the Persian Gulf. It is the declaratory policy of the United States and its North Atlantic allies to respond to conventional attack in Europe with nuclear weapons if the attack cannot be held conventionally. The nuclear weapon and operational nuclear concepts are deeply embedded throughout national military strategy, planning, doctrine, and posture. The Soviet Union similarly is ready and indoctrinated in nuclear war-fighting. During his tenure, Khrushchev threatened nuclear firing some forty-one times.

One must remember the time scale of this problem. It will be with us for a long time, for as far ahead as we can see. The arsenals are now so huge that immense reductions would be needed to cut weapon numbers below the apocalyptic level. The "nuclear winter" study suggests that reductions of about 90 percent would be needed to eliminate the risk that a general exchange could end human life on earth.

Even without the nuclear winter effect, a small fraction of current weapons inventories, discharged against cities, industries, and communications, would be ample to destroy the fabrics, the cultures, and much of the populations of the targeted nations, and leave the survivors living a primitive existence in a poisoned land. Even the wildly optimistic recognize that achieving cuts approaching that magnitude by arms control negotiations would take time measured in decades. More probably, levels will not get that low for the indefinite future; each side will probably insist on retaining final retaliatory forces above the catastrophe point. In any case, this generation, and its children, and its grandchildren, at least, will live in a world with thousands of nuclear weapons, where a few hundreds could destroy civilization.

To avoid catastrophe, then, both sides must refrain from a general exchange of these weapons not just today and tomorrow, but month after month, year after year, decade after decade. Neither one can make that ultimate mistake one single time. These weapons are in the control of men—human beings—with human failings, subject to stress, anger, frustration, lapses of reasoning, ignorance, error, desperation. The control systems for these weapons are of enormous complexity, made up of thousands of men, machines, and operating procedures, subject to failure especially under the stresses of increased alert and, above all, of hostilities. These two nations are bound into an antagonistic relationship. As Seweryn Bialer writes, "The difficulties in U.S.-Soviet relations do not have as their source mutual misperceptions of the two powers by each other. At the heart of the conflict is the real diversity of their interests, a real difference in their evaluation and perception of the international situation, a real diversity of their priorities in approaching the world system, and a real asymmetry in the development of their international appetites and their consciousness of what is possible and obtainable for their respective countries in the international area."[1] The United States and the Soviet Union, in brief, have fundamentally opposed political and social systems. Their objectives conflict in many of the situations where they came in contact. Their interests are global. They do not communicate easily. They distrust one another profoundly. And they are capable of destroying one another.

On that time scale of the indefinite future, with that dependence on fallible human beings, in that condition of built-in antagonism and mutual vulnerability, it is virtually certain that East and West will have confrontations from time to time, and highly probable that some of those confrontations will provoke intense crises. Sooner or later, in one crisis or another, there is at least a substantial risk that even the terrible nuclear threat will not be enough to prevent the outbreak of war between them, somewhere, at some level of intensity. Once it starts, the pressures to continue and to intensify the combat will be very great.

The one great unmistakable boundary would be the introduction of nuclear weapons. The resistance to escalating to the nuclear level will be powerful. That resistance is not secure, however. Under present strategies and doctrines, nuclear forces and concepts are at the heart of the military systems on both sides, and nuclear readiness, both materially and mentally, is high. In the face of combat reverses, or critical obstacles, or failures of control, or, especially, under pressure of fear of imminent hostile nuclear use, the nuclear barrier could fail. From that point, the probability of unlimited escalation would be acute. Lawrence Freedman summarizes the situation concisely: "In the short term, in all conceivable scenarios, only the most appalling set of accidents and miscalculations would cause a full-scale nuclear war. . . . [But] To believe that can go on indefinitely without major disaster requires an optimism unjustified by any historical or political perspective."[2]

Policy Alternatives

How to deal with this threat of catastrophic nuclear war is the dominating problem of the United States and the U.S.S.R., indeed of humanity.

In the military area, there are three broad policies available:

• A nation can try, by pushing new technology to the limit, over decades, to be able both to destroy the opponent and to survive his attacks: a nuclear war-winning policy.

• Or it can try, by designing its forces and plans for a range of nuclear operations, to be able both to achieve national purposes with nuclear weapons or the threat of nuclear weapons and to prevent unlimited escalation: a war-fighting policy, or, more accurately, a nuclear war-controlling policy.

• Or, finally, it can try, by confining the role of its nuclear forces to retaliation against nuclear attack and that alone, to restrict the function of nuclear weapons to the irreducible minimum, rejecting their employment for any purpose whatever except the unique antinuclear deterrent function for which no substitute exists: a policy of minimizing the role of nuclear forces.

The War-Winning Policy

The nuclear war-winning policy is a vision—or a mirage—of the technological future. The vision is of the day when a nation's own forces can enforce its will and assure its survival, no longer ultimately dependent on the enemy's restraint. It is a comforting vision, but it immediately raises three questions: first, can it be done—is it technically feasible; second, cannot the opponent counter it; and, third, what will be the effect of building war-winning capabilities on the nuclear relations between the two countries while the building is going on?

What would be needed to make winning a nuclear war seriously thinkable? We would have to expect to survive as a functioning society, and to be able to destroy the opponent. With weapons of such power, the decisive requirement would be a nearly perfect defense; short of that, "winning" would be a hollow term indeed. In addition to defense, however, in the confident expectation that achievement will, as always, fall short of perfection, other elements of the nuclear forces should demand high development. Key technological objectives would include these:

• ballistic missile defense, almost perfect and nationwide,

• tight defense against air-breathing attack—bombers and cruise missiles,

• the ability to locate and kill, almost simultaneously, ballistic missile submarines and submarine or surface cruise missile carriers at sea,

• the ability to kill, in first or second strike, nearly all the important nuclear targets: the opponent's command and control, his missiles in silos or mobile, his hardened control centers, his aircraft on the field, and submarines in port,

• maintenance of an adequate weapon reserve ample to destroy opposing cities, industries, and economic bases,

• a command and control system able to survive, keep abreast of the situation and in control, and able to make decisions and have them executed during a prolonged period of nuclear war.

Even this list does not cover "suitcase bombs" or other conceivable simple or exotic possibilities.

The technological problems of all this are staggering; the undersecretary of defense for research and engineering described the research and development of just the ballistic missile defense system as having at least eight components, "every single one . . . equivalent to or greater than the Manhattan Project" that developed the atomic bomb. A report for the nonpartisan Congressional Office of Technology Assessment recently concluded that the missile defense technology is "so remote that it should not serve as the basis for public expectation or national policy."

Overall, creating a war-winning posture would require decades, if it could be accomplished at all, even against current threats. But during the development and production period the threat would not stand still. There are techniques and weapons existing today that could be developed to threaten all the war-winning requirements. Ballistic missile defense would be up against a range of already largely developed counter-measures that would enormously enlarge the problem of targeting boosters and warheads; the defense would be vulnerable to antisatellite weapons that would threaten its essential space vehicles; it would be opposed by improved and multiplied offensive weapons. Antisubmarine warfare, with no technical approach in sight to the problem of destroying an entire force of missile submarines at a stroke, would face quieter submarines with longer-range missiles, able to strike from near their bases. Maintaining one's own command and control capacity and destroying the opponent's are the two sides of a very difficult, probably never fully solvable, problem of mutual vulnerability, pushing both sides in the critically dangerous direction of preemptive firing or hair-trigger readiness. An offensive strike able to destroy almost all the potential retaliatory weapons approaches impossibility even when fired in a first-strike with undamaged forces, and would of course be degraded in second-strike after the force had received damage. Such a strike would be up against heavily reinforced silos, defended by point ballistic missile defense, and against mobile and concealable weapons, both ballistic and air-breathing, facing the problems of not surely known accuracy or reliability of attack weapons, unpredictable operational degradation in carrying out a massive, complex, never-tested strike and incalculable mutual interference between attack weapons. To defend against air-breathing weapons that attack from the sea, land, and air in large numbers from all directions, that penetrate at low altitude and have small radar cross sections and thus are hard to detect and attack, and to destroy virtually all of them before they detonate, this, too, would have low probability of success.

In brief, either side's chances are remote of being able to build a true war-winning posture, with an offensive that can disarm the other and a defense that can defeat the other's attack. The technical problems in the aggregate are insoluble or nearly so; the countermeasures are effective and simpler.

What would be the political effect of trying to develop a war-winning capacity? Obviously, a major campaign to erect such a posture would be a mortal threat to the opposing side. That side could not fail to react powerfully with its own programs: countermeasure development, missile and other defenses, and

expanded offensive forces to defeat the first side's defenses.
These, in turn, would further stimulate the first side.

What would be the outcome? There would be years—decades—of intensive research, development, construction, and
deployment on both sides; enormous—incalculable—expendi-
tures of money and human and material resources; periods of
heightened instability when one side or the other achieved
some temporary advantage; then immense new offensive and
defensive systems whose threats would be seen as great but
whose effectiveness would be unpredictable; and no end to
cycles of weapon, antiweapon, antiantiweapon, and so on.

The predictable effect is not some happy day when nuclear
weapons, in Mr. Reagan's phrase, are "impotent and obsolete."
It is instead a time when nations with greatly enlarged forces,
each under increased perceived threat from the other, will see
significant advantage from striking first. They will therefore be
forced to contemplate making a first, preemptive strike or
firing on warning, and will certainly stand at hair-trigger
readiness.

It is interesting to compare the views of two groups of scientists, one Soviet and one U.S., after they examined the problems of "Star Wars" ballistic missile defense. The Soviets say,
". . . it is fair to conclude that its creation will almost certainly
increase the danger of the first (pre-emptive) strike and the
probability of making wrong decisions in a crisis . . . [it] is certain to set off a chain reaction in making more modern weapons
systems, will make the strategic balance more complex and increase the degree of uncertainty in making political and military decisions. . . . As a whole, it should be pointed out that the
very attempt to create a space-based anti-missile system will become a heavily destabilizing factor in increasing the stimulus
for the first pre-emptive strike and the growing danger of
nuclear war. . . . It would open yet another channel of a particularly intensive and unpredictable arms race without any
guarantee of the country's reliable defense against a nuclear
strike."[3]

The American scientists say that if a Star Wars defense could
be built, which they doubt, "We would then have a defense of
stupefying complexity, under total control of a computer program whose proportions defy description, and whose performance will remain a deep mystery until the tragic moment when
it would be called into action. . . . At best, the outcome would

be a defense of precarious reliability, confronted by offensive nuclear forces designed to circumvent and overwhelm it, and a host of 'anti-BMD' [antiballistic missile defense] weapons to attack our armada of space platforms which, in turn, would have to be defended by yet another fleet of anti-anti-BMD weapons. It is difficult to imagine a more hazardous confrontation. . . . We must abandon the illusion that ever more sophisticated technology can, by itself, remove the perils that science and technology have created. We must, instead, recognize the overriding reality of the nuclear age—that we cannot regain safety by sawing off the thin, dry branch on which the Soviets are perched, for we cling to the same branch."[4]

To return to the original question, what use is the nuclear weapon, either fired or as a threat? Insofar as weapons and systems created for and under the war-winning, Star Wars concept are concerned the answer is: none; far from being useful, they are a danger. Nuclear weapons are too powerful, the structure and fabric of nations too fragile, perhaps the global ecosystem too vulnerable, to employ nuclear weapons "successfully." Technology cannot overcome this reality. The weapons of the war-winning policy will, as threats, produce not nuclear safety but enhanced danger; actually fired, they will not prevent unimaginable disaster. It is the wrong path to follow.

The War-Controlling (War-Fighting) Policy

A nuclear war-controlling policy, based on a concept of controlled nuclear war-fighting, differs fundamentally from a war-winning policy. The heart of the difference is that war-controlling recognizes that large-scale nuclear war will inevitably be mutually disastrous. Its approach is not to deny that ultimate reality. Rather it seeks to prevent full-scale escalation, while using the threat or if necessary the firing of nuclear forces to achieve national purposes: preventing war, preventing escalation, preventing conventional defeat, obtaining local success, perhaps compelling desired actions.

War-controlling, broadly speaking, is current Soviet and U.S. policy, but their concepts differ. For the Soviet side, one can infer a hierarchy of objectives that appear to govern their strategy. They seek first: peace; failing that: conventional hostilities; failing that: nuclear operations that do not strike the Soviet Union; and finally, that failing: full-scale nuclear war. They would move up this scale only as driven by the other side's actions, imminent preparations, or successes, as lured by real or apparent opportunities, or as swept along by events. They are fully conscious of the threat of catastrophe; pressures against these major escalations—especially peace to war and conventional to nuclear—would be powerful. Within each level of hostilities, however, the Soviet Union would be governed by traditional, conventional military concepts. They can be expected, that is, to go all out for the victory. Their nuclear targeting, whether at theatre or general level, would seek to destroy military, support, industrial, and governmental elements in the targeted zones as thoroughly and rapidly as possible.

U.S. concepts are more elaborate. The United States also, of course, seeks peace and is aware of the danger of nuclear disaster. Two factors, however, make the United States depend more heavily on the leverage of the nuclear weapon. First is the location of major U.S. allies and interests in Eurasia, accessible to Soviet conventional military power. Second is the perceived operational superiority of that Soviet conventional power in a number of key areas of possible conflict, especially Central Europe and the Persian Gulf, a superiority that has been accepted as an article of faith in the West for a generation. Together, under the war-controlling policy, these elements appear to require the United States, in order to defend its essential interests, to be able to use the threat or, ultimately, the actual firing of nuclear weapons, while avoiding escalation to an all-out, mutually suicidal general exchange.

Thus the U.S. nuclear escalatory scale can be divided conceptually into tactical (battlefield), counterforce (against military targets, nuclear and conventional), and countervalue (industrial, economic, national leadership targets). Operationally, the planning creates a wide range of attack "options," that is, alternative targeting and attack plans from among which the national command authority (the president, or his successor) can choose at the time of firing, depending on the situation then existing. The options are gathered into categories of major, selected, limited, and regional attack options, varying from a few weapons to thousands. The intent is to be able to deter hostile military action, or if necessary to meet it, over the full range of foreseen possibilities, by precalculated nuclear responses of progressively increasing weight, aimed at systematically determined sets of targets such as nuclear forces, support elements, resources, communications, and controls. Planning also provides for retaining secure nuclear forces in reserve, able to threaten cataclysmic destruction, available for negotiating leverage even during and after controlled nuclear exchanges. The objectives of this so-called "countervailing" strategy is to deter or if necessary meet any hostile military action, so that the opponent will not be able to obtain anything describable as victory, or any advantage that would justify his losses, in any geographical location, at any level of intensity, and over whatever time period operations continue.

To determine the utility of nuclear weapons under this war-controlling (or "war-fighting" or "escalation control") policy, several questions need answers:

• Can nuclear weapons attacks produce usable military advantage?

• Can nuclear war, once started, be controlled, be limited?

• What is the effect of war-controlling policy and forces on the nuclear threat (deterrence)?

• What is the effect on the U.S.-U.S.S.R. relationship of *building* such war-fighting forces and systems?

Taking these questions in sequence, one starts with plain, traditional military utility. Is there military advantage to be gained from introducing nuclear weapons into hostilities? Are they of military use? Alternative situations to consider might include: use of nuclear weapons to stop conventional attack, say in Europe or the Persian Gulf; strikes against hostile nuclear forces to limit the damage they could do in return; and attacks against specific key target systems—command and control systems, transportation, supply, and industrial focal points, or particular military elements (e.g., Soviet military forces facing China)—to reduce, disorganize, or threaten the opponent's combat power. In brief, is there military gain to be had from using nuclear weapons against conventional forces, nuclear forces, or selected target systems?

Using U.S. and NATO nuclear forces to stop Warsaw Pact conventional attack on the Central European area, if conventional defense were unable to stem it, is NATO's declaratory policy and has received much study. There are questions of feasibility; in the presumed rapidly moving successful Soviet

attack, including, probably, attacks against NATO's theater nuclear forces, it is questionable whether NATO's allied and national political and military control and release system could
function quickly and effectively enough to launch coordinated
tactical strikes. Assuming operational effectiveness, however,
the scale of the strikes would probably be large.

Computerized games have been run using a range of scenarios, weapons, and targeting, trying to get some feel for possible outcomes. The results must, of course, be understood as
at best rough approximations. In general, in various games, the
range of immediate fatalities (i.e., not counting those who
would die in a short time from radiation, trauma, or illness)
could run from perhaps 2 million to 100 million. The lowest of
those losses come from a highly unrealistic case where NATO
used tactical weapons (7,000 weapons, 1 to 25 kilotons) on ad-
vancing Warsaw Pact forces, very close to the front, avoiding
cities, and the Pact did not reply with nuclear weapons. A
slightly more valid "engaged battle," with 8,000 weapons going
in both directions (2 kilotons to 1 megaton), to a depth limited
to 40 kilometers on each side, still with tightly controlled avoidance of cities, would produce 3 to 4 million quick dead. If the
Pact used 1,500 2-KT to 20-MT weapons, more deeply, West
European dead would rise to 35 million. There is no natural
limit point; 100 million dead are within range of the possible.
Material damage would be proportionate.

Those kinds of scenarios are based on the notion that tactical
nuclear weapons are only a higher-powered artillery, that their
use can be embodied in conventional military operations, coordinated with traditional fire and movement, advance and
retreat. Nuclear weapons, however, are not conventional weapons. They act at a different level of violence. They blow holes
impartially in both attack and defense. They destroy the channels that transmit information on the situation and that control
the forces. The idea that it will be possible to exercise knowledgeable control of nuclear operations over time, during nuclear exchanges, is simply not valid.

A different conceptual approach is to recognize that the tactical nuclear forces are really minor strategic forces, capable
only of destroying targets, and to tailor the forces to the target
set. Something less than 2,000 targets on each side, without hitting cities, would suffice: say, 150 airfields, 600 missile sites, 700

transport bottlenecks, 90 division assembly points, and 700 company size units. Hitting such a target list would cripple the other side's air/ground attack or defense. The tactical nuclear system and posture could be designed to be able to destroy such a target system, and to be able to survive to do so on second strike after sustaining an attack on both its weapons and control system, without seeking the impossible goal of control for a prolonged period. (The Pershing II and Ground Launched Cruise Missiles [GLCM] recently deployed in Europe, it should be noted, show little sign of such rational design. Their numbers are arbitrary, unrelated to targets, and they are themselves relatively easy targets, chosen without giving adequate weight to their vulnerability.)

Using either the superartillery or the ministrategic plan, in a standard scenario, the Warsaw Pact attacks conventionally into Central Europe, i.e., into West Germany, and breaks through the NATO defenses. NATO responds with nuclear weapons, and uses enough of them, on a broad enough set of targets, to cripple the attack. The Warsaw Pact responds with nuclear weapons. Presumably, under their existing doctrines, their target priorities are: first, NATO's nuclear resources in the theater (West Germany, France, the United Kingdom, the Low Countries, Italy); second, military forces, command and control, support structure, lines of communication—seaports and the other transportation foci. There will be death in millions, wounded and sick in additional millions, enormous material destruction, loss of organized control of military forces and other governmental systems in attacked areas—in general, chaos. Chaos in the battle area on both sides. And all that chaos could result from one or two salvos, fired in hours or even minutes.

There are many variations on the scenarios. The Warsaw Pact could start the nuclear phase itself, in the conviction, say, that NATO was on the verge of striking. This would produce substantial losses in NATO's nuclear capabilities in the theater; there is, unfortunately, that advantage to striking first. Remaining and external nuclear forces, however, would still be ample to create NATO's share of the chaos, by escalation if necessary.

It is, then, very probably possible to wreck a conventional attack into Central Europe by using battlefield and theater nuclear weapons on a large scale, accepting staggering human loss and material destruction. The problem is that wrecking the attack with nuclear weapons simultaneously makes the conventional battle irrelevant. Once there is nuclear use, the struggle becomes a nuclear war, not a war of conventional forces. The sole concern would then be what the nuclear weapons were doing—how close and how inevitable was complete destruction. No one will care where the conventional battlefront is, or whether it even exists. The war, to the extent it is under any control, will consist of manipulating the threat of ultimate catastrophe.

A substantial exchange with appalling loss and chaotic conditions in the theater is the minimum realistic expectation—destruction rather than defense of our NATO allies. Further, as will be discussed later, limiting nuclear operations once started is improbable indeed. The outcome to be expected, with high probability, is unlimited escalation and global disaster.

There are other theaters where the use of nuclear weapons could be considered. The most prominent possibility at present is the Persian Gulf, where two U.S. presidents have declared the oil flow from the oil producing nations a vital interest of the United States.

As an example, a common Persian Gulf scenario puts U.S. ground, naval, and air forces in the area, at the end of a long supply line. The ground forces are in a beachhead at the head of the Gulf; the aircraft are operating from aircraft carriers, from Diego Garcia in the Indian Ocean and possibly from Turkish, Egyptian, or Arabian peninsula bases. Strategic Air Command aircraft could even intervene from the Western Pacific. The Soviet forces are making a ground and air attack, based in the Caucasus, through Iran to the Gulf. The U.S. objective is, ideally, to keep the oil flowing and, failing that, to keep the U.S.S.R. from overrunning the oil countries. The U.S.S.R. objective is to drive the U.S. forces out of the Gulf and the oil countries, and to control the flow of Gulf oil. Is there military advantage to either side from using nuclear weapons?

From the U.S. side, potential nuclear targets for blunting or stopping the Soviet advance are the restricted Iranian communications, with narrow roads and numerous bridges and tunnels through the Elburz and the Zagros mountain ranges, and the Soviet base structure in the Caucasus and the Soviet southern military districts. The Soviets would consider hitting the U.S. beachhead, the limited U.S. base structure, and the oil installations.

There would be little operational incentive for the United States to use nuclear weapons. Used against communications in the mountains, nuclear weapons would add little to the effectiveness in that terrain of conventional operations, and the almost certain Soviet nuclear response would strike a more vulnerable and more decisive U.S. target list; obviously, the U.S.S.R. with nuclear weapons could turn off the oil tap entirely, largely destroy the U.S. forces and bases, and thus unhinge the U.S. position. Used against the southern U.S.S.R. itself, on a scale to cripple the attack, nuclear weapons would immediately escalate the war to the full strategic level, with the existence of both countries at imminent risk.

From the Soviet standpoint, the campaign should be manageable conventionally, and if not going well could be reinforced and built up as they saw fit. The oil is not vital for the U.S.S.R.; conventional bombing could make it unavailable to the West. There is thus no apparent necessity for the Soviet Union to break the nuclear barrier, and nothing to be gained thereby to balance the losses, damage, and risk of escalation from a U.S. nuclear response.

In the Gulf as in Central Europe, then, nuclear weapons promise no military gain but expose the user to immediate great loss and damage and to high risk of catastrophe. Similar conditions apply around the periphery of the Soviet Zone. Admiral Noel Gayler, USN (Ret), for several years Commander in Chief of the Pacific (CINCPAC) theater, set his large, interservice planning staff to examining his immense theater for possible advantageous uses of nuclear weapons. Assuming nuclear response, that is to say, a two-sided nuclear exchange, they found none. Gayler writes, "After thorough study by the CINCPAC Joint Staff, it was evident to me that there is no sensible first use of nuclear weapons in any area from the Middle East around to Northeast Asia, or at sea, or, indeed, anywhere else."[5]

There is another point to note. The war-controlling policy could cause our military and political leaders to rely on being able to use nuclear weapons to shore up conventional operations in emergency, and therefore to take ill-advised risks with the conventional forces. This thought stimulated one phrase maker to refer to the Rapid Deployment Force as "a portable Dien Bien Phu."

A feature of war-controlling nuclear operational planning emphasized in the last decade has been to try to identify specific target sets that could be individually attacked, whose destruction would have decisive or at least substantial influence on the outcome, but which would be palpably different from an all-out city-busting strike and would thus not necessarily incite an all-out response.

Some examples are: a Soviet attack on U.S. land-based, strategic Minuteman missiles, using a fraction of their high-accuracy, silo-killing warheads but destroying nearly all our "quick response, hard target killing" capacity; an attack by either side on the other's command and control system, intended to leave the nuclear forces disorganized and unable to carry out coordinated operations; a U.S. attack on Soviet forces facing China, to expose the Soviet Union to the threat of Chinese invasion; attacks on specific supply, resource, and recovery systems: petroleum, transportation, electrical power, etc.; and a "decapitating" attack to destroy the opponent's fabric of government: officials, channels, institutions. Planners are understood to be trying to find key targets where a very small number of nuclear weapons could seriously unhinge a major conventional attack in Central Europe. There has been even some advocacy of "ethnic targeting," aimed at killing Great Russians and sparing ethnic minorities, so that Russians would not control the postwar state.

These are all "war-fighting" targets, whose goal is military advantage, an attempt to subsume nuclear use under traditional military concepts. The nuclear weapon, however, will not fit into the classic pattern. After any or all of the attacks listed in the preceding paragraph, the nuclear forces of the attacked nation could still destroy the attacking nation, perhaps raggedly if leadership and communications damage had been extensive, but thoroughly, and could themselves be destroyed in return by the original user of nuclear weapons. Such mutual vulnerability to unimaginable catastrophe is not a strategic theory, but an objective fact, a result of the nature of the nuclear weapons and the size of the U.S. and Soviet nuclear arsenals. This ultimate reality will be the governing consideration, indeed the only significant consideration, if the United States and U.S.S.R. break the nuclear barrier. The outcome of a silo-to-silo missile exchange, conducted like a long-range artillery duel, will be entirely peripheral. The physical impact of the destruction of most U.S. Minutemen by a fraction of Soviet SS-18s, for example, will neither remove the capacity of each nation to destroy the other nor even eliminate the ability of the United States to execute a range of less-than-all-out nuclear responses. Like other limited, controlled attacks, it will generate no usable military advantage. It need not deflect U.S. decision making.

This basic inutility of nuclear weapons as combat tools is difficult to comprehend, conditioned as the world is to millennia of prenuclear warfare. When the nuclear weapon came into being, forty years ago, it was natural, even irresistible, to treat it as only one more, if immense, step in the long history of weapons development, a follow-on to such decisive but finally manageable changes as the stirrup, gunpowder, the aircraft. Even after forty years of study, it is not yet driven fully into human understanding that the nuclear weapon is not a step in development, or even a revolution, but has taken us into a totally new era where nuclear conflict between states has lost all relevance to their political objectives.

Thus it is commonplace to hear that, if conventional defense is failing in Central Europe, NATO will be "forced" to use nuclear weapons. As noted above, the effect of supporting failing conventional operations with nuclear weapons would be to add a nuclear disaster to a conventional reverse, and to create a prohibitive risk of unlimited escalation and global catastrophe—an irrational, virtually suicidal act. And yet, under classic, conventional, pre-nuclear-revolution concepts that govern much debate and action among leaders as well as the public, such decisions can still seem correct.

Some years ago, in a small conference in the situation room in the basement of the White House, Henry Kissinger, then President Nixon's assistant for national security, asked the acting chairman of the Joint Chiefs of Staff if, were the Central European front failing, the Joint Chiefs would advise the president to release nuclear weapons for use there. The general's snap answer, without a moment's pause, was not "Yes" or "No," but "Of course." Kissinger pursued the question, asking what good would the nuclears do; what would the chiefs expect to accomplish with them? The answer was (approximately), "Nuclears would be all we had left to use." This is a sound, pre-nuclear decision; at the crisis, the good general should bring all his forces to bear. In the nuclear era it reveals a failure to recognize the nuclear revolution.

Another example can be deduced from President Nixon's *Foreign Policy* report to the Congress in February 1970: "Should the President," he wrote, "in the event of nuclear attack, be left with the single option of ordering the mass destruction of enemy civilians, in the face of the certainty that it would be followed by the mass slaughter of Americans?" Robert Jervis provides the answer: "In a crisis or to respond to a major Soviet provocation, the United States certainly needs alternatives to passivity or an all-out strike. But it has had them for at least twenty years. The missiles need not be fired all at once. The common claim that an American president might be left with only the choice between humiliation and holocaust is silly. If the command, control, and communication (C^3) system survives, there are any number of actions that can be taken to increase the costs to the Soviets and the risks to both sides. The targets the United States would want to hit probably would be military ones, but *pressure would not be brought to bear through the traditional route of gaining military advantage. Instead, the strikes would both demonstrate resolve and generate risks that further escalation will occur* [emphasis supplied]. . . . As long as the societies of both sides are vulnerable, a crisis or a superpower war will be like a game of chicken."[6] In brief, limited nuclear exchanges between the United States and the U.S.S.R., unprecedented though the death and destruction they cause would be, would not change the fundamental strategic situation. That situation is that each can destroy the other. Each will continue to be able to do so after limited exchanges. The specific limited targets chosen are of minor significance; there are numerous military, noncity choices. The limited exchanges are essentially signals. President Nixon's rhetorical question suggests that he had not absorbed reality.

American target planning of recent years has produced a large number of alternative operational choices options from which the president might choose for launching nuclear strikes. Each option has been worked out thoroughly and laboriously: weapon selection, target selection, timing, force requirements, estimated results. The planning shows the problems and the requirements of each option and set of options;

predictably it has produced a demand for more weapons. The basic purpose, however, is to find target packages and make ready to hit them if ordered, so that the president, in great crisis, can be presented a huge menu of ready strikes, and so that, if and when he chooses one or more of them, it or they can be promptly executed (the state of the command and control system permitting).

But no one can tell what strikes would deter the Soviets, or stimulate escalation, or lead to termination of the exchange. The system requires the president, or his successor if he has been killed, to choose among this smorgasbord of options while under incredible stress, although the planners are unable to establish reasonable preferences in calm peacetime. The ultimate futility of the exercise is that the choice of targets is not fundamentally significant. At base, it does not matter whether "limited" nuclear attacks are aimed at missile silos, troops on the Chinese border, or petroleum supplies. What limited strikes can accomplish, and all they can accomplish, as Jervis points out, is to demonstrate resolve and to generate risks of further escalation.

Even that limited purpose stands on a dubious foundation. One of the wisest students of the nuclear problem is the British historian Michael Howard. He has contended that U.S. planners are "pushing precision into an area where it can't survive." He was asked by a group of U.S. analysts about what targets to hit to overcome the U.S.S.R. in a nuclear war, how to use nuclear weapons to weaken and frighten Russia without unleashing the holocaust. According to Thomas Powers, Howard replied along the following lines: "Didn't they understand what they were talking about? Nuclear weapons can't be used like that! The devastation would inevitably blur the outlines of any plan. The Russians would have no way of knowing what was coming next. The planners in Washington could forget all their subtleties about escalation dominance. What they would get is apocalyptic horror."[7]

Howard was arguing that limited nuclear war would be uncontrollable, that once started on nuclear use—even just to demonstrate resolve and threaten escalation—the process would go out of control. Almost everyone agrees that all-out, city-busting war would be an unimaginable catastrophe. Would limited nuclear war, in any form, lead irresistibly to general war? Can limited nuclear war be controlled? In other words, is the war-controlling policy operationally workable at all?

Controlling Limited Nuclear War

The war-controlling policy argues, basically, that nuclear war between the United States and the Soviet Union could be kept limited, restricted, controlled. Could a nuclear exchange in fact be held to the detonation of tens, or even hundreds, of nuclear weapons, even though each side would still have thousands of weapons ready for use and would still be capable of literally destroying the other?

It is most improbable. Consider the situation of the leaders and decision makers on both sides during a limited exchange. First, they would be under unprecedented, almost unendurable stress—pressure of events, pressure of time, pressure of apprehension, pressure of fatigue. Stress makes human thinking more primitive, and it impels to impulsive action, the worst possible state for deciding the fate of the world. Second, there would be a flood of information coming in, but it would be ambiguous, delayed, partial. Picking out the essential facts would be hard or impossible. The result: the two sides would be operating on different information received at different times. They would not be fighting the same war. Third, each side would be functioning under the corroding fear that the other might launch a general strike at any moment. Both would be on hair triggers and thus apt to fire on misinformation, misinterpretation, or error. Fourth, each side would similarly have in mind the shining hope that a major, all-out strike might succeed, might, conceivably, bring things to a close in its favor—in brief, that a full-scale attack might not inevitably produce absolute catastrophe in return. It would be a critically dangerous temptation when stress became unendurable.

The two sides, inevitably, have different operational concepts. Soviet doctrine contemplates that if nuclear war does happen, they will prosecute it without restraint, whether at theater or global level, aiming to limit damage to themselves and accomplish all they can militarily. Their concept is to attack large numbers of military and urban-industrial targets simultaneously, with prompt, heavy strikes. American doctrine tries to maintain an element of deterrence even after nuclear war has commenced ("intrawar deterrence"), by maintaining a wide range of attacks in readiness, from among which political authority can choose the most effective for the actual situation at the time, by refraining, initially, from massive urban attack, and by holding out for bargaining leverage a reserve force with enough weapons to destroy the U.S.S.R. by urban-industrial attacks.

The two systems, obviously, do not blend. The Soviet system rejects limited nuclear war. The U.S. system is based upon it, but requires that both governments maintain control of their forces, select target sets on the basis of reasonably compatible criteria, keep accurate and current track of the situation, keep their military operations in careful phase with political strategy, communicate their positions clearly to one another, and correctly evaluate the other side's position. The U.S. approach requires two to tango; the Soviets will not dance that dance.

There is serious doubt whether either of the two governments has the physical abilities to control nuclear forces in times of high tension, conventional war, and limited nuclear war: doubts both as to what risk there is of firing the weapons or escalating without central authority, and as to whether command systems could operate under nuclear combat damage.

The first risk, that of firing by local initiative, is clouded by the common metaphor "push the button," implying that these immense forces, on both sides, are unitary objects lying inert until given a governmental order and then instantly and precisely controlled by that order. In fact, of course, the problem is not like flipping a light switch. These are large, complex forces of thousands of men, machines, and communications. They are, necessarily, organized into many elements and tied into various hierarchical command patterns. They are subject to a range of orders, standard operating procedures, and controls designed to accomplish two purposes: to prevent firing when not wanted, and to assure firing when it is wanted.

In calm times, the negative control is clearly stronger; problems, errors, equipment failures, loss of communications, etc., would be checked and rechecked at all levels. It is almost inconceivable that there could be inadvertent launch in normal times. As tension built up between the superpowers, however, and especially as the nuclear forces were ordered into advanced stages of alert, and, of course, even more notably if conventional hostilities were taking place—overwhelmingly if some nuclear firing were going on—nuclear forces would inevitably follow the pattern of all military forces; leaders at all levels would make every effort to avoid being caught unready. Organizations and individuals would get on hair triggers. The forces on the two sides would stimulate each other; all information of one side's alert measures would drive the other to higher tension and readiness. All the safety factors and control rules would be pushed to or beyond the limit.

In this situation, error, equipment failure, communication failure, most acutely information of increased alerts of the other side's forces or misinformation of a hostile launch, unauthorized subordinate initiative—some combination of these could trigger, somewhere in the system, unordered launching. And after initial launching, authorized or not, pressure to fire would be powerful and control reduced.

The problem of combat damage is more obvious, both the death of leaders and destruction of communications and equipment for obtaining information and giving directions. These control and information systems are intrinsically more vulnerable than the weapon systems themselves. Given even limited nuclear attacks, existing systems would strain just to carry out their basic mission, i.e., to establish temporary command channels to trigger large-scale retaliation. It is unrealistic to think they would remain workable, able to control complex operations, over a period of days and weeks. And this is unlikely to change, even with considerable investments in more hardened and redundant control systems, because of the inescapable relative vulnerability of control systems and the limited number and unreliable protection of the key political and military authorities. Desmond Ball, the noted nuclear strategist, concludes, "The capability to exercise strict control and coordination would inevitably be lost relatively early in the nuclear exchange."[8]

Finally, it must also be stressed that no one, on either side, has devised a plan or a process or a mechanism for stopping nuclear exchange once started.

For limited nuclear war to remain limited, then—to stop, that is, short of complete catastrophe—the two sides would have to work in parallel. They would have to do so with different information, different weapons and controls, different operational concepts and plans and mechanisms, under appalling pressure of event and time, with diametrically opposed objectives, with the continued existence of both nations literally in the balance. Right in the middle of substantial nuclear exchanges and the resulting death, destruction, chaos, and loss of central control of all or parts of the forces, they would have to work out and put into effect mutually tolerable operational limits—mutually accepted and observed limits, that is, on the kinds of weapons they used and the kinds and locations of targets they fired at. Further, and this is even less conceivable, still in mid-exchange, still under intolerable stress, still with decisive time intervals measured in minutes, they would have to arrive somehow at an agreed outcome, a stopping point, short of the ultimate exchange.

It is beyond belief. Robert McNamara has studied the nuclear problems over the past two decades. As secretary of defense under two presidents, he felt and observed intimately for seven years the pressures and realities of nuclear responsibility. He was driven to this conclusion: "It is inconceivable to me, as it has been to others who have studied the matter, that 'limited' nuclear wars would remain limited—any decision to use nuclear weapons would imply a high probability of the same cataclysmic consequences as a total nuclear exchange."[9]

Desmond Ball is crisper. Controlled nuclear war, says Ball, is a "chimera."[10]

Deterrence

In this nuclear age, in the state of nuclear abundance and nuclear parity, the driving objective on both sides is not victory but deterrence. The word "deterrence," it should be noted, has become mushy from much careless use. We need to specify deterrence of what, under what circumstances. On the Soviet side nuclear deterrence appears to be aimed specifically at deterrence of nuclear attack. The U.S.S.R. has declared it will not be the first to use nuclear weapons. Concepts of Soviet preemption seem to apply only to situations where they believe U.S. nuclear attack is certain and imminent. The Soviet threat, if nuclear weapons are used, is of heavy, large-scale, general attack, at least throughout the engaged theater of operations, perhaps globally.

On the U.S. side, the objective is to deter any aggression, conventional or nuclear, that could lead to nuclear war. The "countervailing," war-controlling policy requires the United States to have forces and plans in readiness for a variety of operations, hoping that the U.S.S.R. would recognize that no type of aggression would produce victory, however they defined victory. The deterrence sought would be that of having U.S. nuclear forces deter not just massive attacks on cities, but also other major but limited nuclear or conventional attacks: on U.S. strategic nuclear forces, for example, or, with conventional forces, on Central Europe or the Gulf. And a further goal is deterrence by "escalation control," maintaining forces and posture to convince the Soviets, even during limited nuclear exchanges, that there is no further intermediate level of nuclear intensity to which they might escalate, where they would be successful.

Escalation control is simply impractical. It requires a marked and recognized nuclear superiority, and not only overall nuclear superiority but superiority at each level of intensity, each theater, and each kind of target system. Neither side need permit nor will permit the other to achieve anything like such complete superiority.

The American approach to deterrence is in large part a leftover from the days of, first, U.S. nuclear monopoly, and, later, of great superiority. Then it was plausible, as the phrase went, to place "primary but not complete" dependence on nuclear forces for military security. Today, when both sides have immense nuclear arsenals, it is profoundly dangerous, sooner or later disastrous, to overload the nuclear forces, to depend on them for all-purpose deterrence. The threat of nuclear response to a variety of nonnuclear attacks is indeed a very powerful deterrent, but it is an unacceptable risk to rely on such "extended" nuclear deterrence succeeding invariably, for the indefinite future, over the whole range of U.S.-Soviet conflict, when one failure, whether in the first or nth East-West crisis, would spell disaster.

The force of nuclear deterrence comes not from the threat of losing a battle, a campaign, or a force of intercontinental ballistic missiles (ICBMs), not even of losing a few million people. Such considerations would have been decisive in the prenuclear era, when decisions of peace and war were made, at least in theory, on the basis of national gain and loss. Today, no conceivable gain could remotely balance the losses. The possible specific outcomes of specific attacks, conventional or limited nuclear, are dwarfed by the threat of essentially complete destruction of all the targeted countries—their fabrics, their cultures, most of their populations, nearly all that the populations and their forefathers had built—plus calamitous secondary effects on the other nations of the world, and possibly, if

Carl Sagan and his "nuclear winter" colleagues are correct, other yet-undiscovered catastrophic effects of nuclear exchange emerge, the end of life on earth.

What makes that appalling threat convincingly real is not the notion that leaders on either side would coldly opt for all-out nuclear war, expecting their countries to gain, on balance, or at least to lose less. It is rather the entirely rational, historically justified fear that as crisis, confrontation, hostilities occurred and intensified, events themselves would take charge and inexorably drive governments, armed forces, and people, like a hurricane, to the holocaust.

It can be argued that restricting nuclear deterrence to deterring nuclear war and only nuclear war—by, say, a policy of no-first-use of nuclear weapons—would make conventional war more probable. There is some truth in this; presumably some actions to strengthen nonnuclear deterrence of conventional war would be indicated. However:

• This objection equates the consequences of nuclear war and conventional war. Nuclear war and conventional war are not comparable. No citizen of this century needs to be reminded that conventional war causes terrible tragedy. It is, however, tragedy that can be survived. Consider Germany, at the center of and on the losing side of the two great wars of this century, split in two by the second, and yet, today, functioning ably and powerfully. The culture of Goethe survives.

If nuclear weapons are used, however, there is a prohibitively high probability of unimaginable and irreparable damage. Risking nuclear catastrophe for a marginal reduction of conventional deterrence is not rational.

• The force of nuclear deterrence of less than nuclear attack is in any case eroding, as the suicidal result of using nuclears under any circumstances becomes more and more widely understood. To be convincing, the means of deterrence must be proportionate to the objective sought; threatening suicide for a less than mortal issue inevitably raises suspicion that the threat is a bluff.

• Threatening nuclear weapons to deter nonnuclear operations asserts that nuclear weapons are usable in such circumstances. It intrinsically lowers the nuclear threshold and makes nuclear firing more thinkable and thus more probable.

• The overriding defect of nuclear deterrence of conventional hostilities is that it irresistibly nuclearizes the national strategies, the armed forces, and the national security apparatus. With it, nuclear use is always the dominant military consideration. Military education and training, military hardware, plans, deployments, operations—the whole military/security machinery— are based on the concept that nuclear weapons may be brought into conventional operation at any time. Nuclear capabilities are built into nearly all elements of the armed forces; nuclear operations are trained for; nuclear readiness is kept high. Military commanders will expect nuclear support when it appears necessary on military grounds; they will call for it when in difficulties. National leaders, under appalling stresses, in the fog of war, receiving a drumfire of demands for nuclear operations, conditioned like the military to nuclear use, will be under enormous pressure to issue the nuclear release.

In brief, using nuclear weapons for general deterrence keeps readiness for and expectation of nuclear use high, in the military and in the governmental control apparatus. In this climate, under the war-controlling policy, the probability of *any* substantial U.S.-U.S.S.R. hostilities becoming nuclear is high.

To repeat, nuclear deterrence of nuclear attack is essential; no other sanction is of a scope and force commensurate with the nuclear threat. Threatening a range of limited nuclear options under the war-controlling policy, however, adds little or nothing to the strength of deterrence of nuclears, and threatening nuclear response to nonnuclear attack under that policy makes nuclear war the probable outcome of any U.S.-U.S.S.R. hostilities.

A further aspect of the war-controlling policy is its damaging effect on U.S.-Soviet relations. War-controlling accepts nuclear weapons as usable, as legitimate, if terrible, weapons. From the standpoint of the opponent, that conveys a willingness, ultimately, to destroy the fabric, the culture, and the people of his or her nation. It assumes and it perpetuates an irrevocable hostility. Further, war-fighting nuclear forces are not procured for a set target list; they are intended to engage the opponent's forces and therefore they are built to match those forces. The two sides thus inevitably stimulate each other; it is the basis for an open-ended nuclear arms race with no natural limit. There is no point where enough is enough. Also, the war-fighting concept of nuclear forces threatening opposed nuclear forces demands high readiness and quick response, which raises the risk of unintended or inadequately studied launching. Profound hostility, a continuing arms race, and high readiness for nuclear attack are a dangerous combination for two nations capable of destroying each other.

In summary, the war-controlling policy produces a rationale for very large nuclear forces, held at high readiness, with strategies and plans for a variety of attacks. The foregoing discussion, however, argues that none of these attacks, actually launched, would produce any usable military advantage, that nuclear war, however initiated, cannot be controlled, that nuclear deterrence under the war-controlling policy increases the risk that any U.S.-U.S.S.R. hostilities would become nuclear, and that the war-fighting forces and strategy exacerbate hostility and stimulate the nuclear arms race.

The war-controlling policy requires a range of nuclear war-fighting capabilities: counterforce weapons capable of destroying hard targets, control systems able to function through prolonged periods of nuclear exchange, and plans, preparations, training, and material for a spectrum of nuclear operations and of simultaneous continuing conventional operations. The discussion herein argues, however, that much of this is excessive, that in most instances it increases the nuclear danger rather than controlling it, and that the only valid use for nuclear forces is to deter the other side's use of nuclear weapons.

The policy here recommended is that of minimizing the role of nuclear forces, as discussed in the following section. It is within that policy that nuclear forces find their limited but vital role.

Minimizing the Nuclear Role

The policy of minimizing the nuclear role rests on the dominating mutual interest of the United States and U.S.S.R. in preventing nuclear war between them. Without general nuclear war they are fundamentally secure; with it they face the prohibitively high probability of national destruction, of unimaginable catastrophe. Preventing nuclear war must be the highest priority task for both; in George Kennan's words, ". . . there is no issue at stake in our political relations with the Soviet Union— no hope, no fear, nothing to which we aspire, nothing we would like to avoid—which could conceivably be worth a nuclear war."[11]

The ideal would be to eliminate all nuclear weapons, but the difficulties in so doing appear insurmountable, at least for a long time to come. Weapon technology is widely known. Weapon concealment is possible. A cheating party, with a number of weapons, would have an unchallengeable advantage over a complying party with none. An organization able to ensure weapon elimination, globally, would have to have many characteristics of a world government, and have greater right of search and seizure than we accord our own government.

The day may come when the peoples of the world are ready to give up substantial elements of their personal and national freedom of action in order to overcome the risk of nuclear holocaust. Clearly, however, the time is not yet. Also, unilateral nuclear disarmament, by either superpower, exposing itself to destruction by any nuclearly armed nation, is far from present political reality. Finally, as discussed above, negotiated arms control agreements that would reduce the two arsenals below the capacity for mutual catastrophe are highly unlikely for the foreseeable future.

In these circumstances, there is no wholly secure outcome to the U.S.-U.S.S.R. nuclear dilemma. The most nearly satisfactory solution within reach is, at base, a redirection of thinking.

The key changes are in minds rather than in arsenals. Governments, militaries, and publics need to understand and accept nuclear reality, specifically that—given nuclear arms on both sides—there is no national gain from any firing of nuclear weapons, that there are no circumstances whatever where first nuclear use is rational, that nuclear weapons are unusable for achieving human or national purposes, that their only function is to deter an opponent from nuclear firing, and that that function exists only because there is no other known measure available of even remotely adequate power and reach to be a convincing counterthreat to, and thus a deterrent of, the use of nuclear weapons.

The basic conceptual change needed is to abandon the futile search for a useful role for nuclear weapons in threat or in firing, and to concentrate on withdrawing them, as far as possible, from the U.S.-U.S.S.R. power equation. It demands a deep understanding of the truth that if you cannot defend conventionally, you cannot defend at all. The goal is stable, confident, mutual nuclear deterrence, strong enough to hold in periods of tension, in crisis, even during conventional hostilities, even—this is the limiting case—during conventional hostilities when one or the other side is losing.

A prerequisite, clearly, is a strong nuclear deterrent posture, able to retaliate with catastrophic effect after any nuclear attack the opponent could make. This removes any incentive for a preemptive strike. A further essential, for stability, is that the possessor of the deterrent have solid confidence in it, be sure that he could retaliate effectively even if massively attacked. This removes any incentive to "use-it-before-you-lose-it." The policy imperative that follows is that each side not only must be sure of its own deterrent strength, but also should avoid measures that threaten the opponent's deterrent. The more acute our threat to their deterrent forces, the more grounds we give them to be hyperalert and trigger-happy, apt to fire on misinformation, technical failure, error, or fear, and the more they are driven to build more and more weapons. Their threat to us produces the same effect in reverse. For both, the less secure one is, the less secure the other is.

A policy of minimizing the nuclear role has to be implemented by a range of policies and measures. These are to establish and make convincing, both to the opponent and to one's own leaders, forces, and people, that using nuclear weapons for military operational purposes is eliminated from one's consideration, is no longer legitimate. Such policies and measures should include:

• *No First Use*—a declaration that the nation would not be the first to fire nuclear weapons in any future hostilities. This policy is discussed below.

• *No Immediate Response*—a declaration that the nation would not retaliate against an incoming nuclear strike until it had determined the source of the attack, the size of the attack, and the intentions of the attacker. This would include renouncing the option of launching on warning. Such a policy would respond to an accident, a mistake, firing by a third party or some human or mechanical failure on either side. With a secure retaliatory force, it is not necessary to make a snap response. Ample retaliation remains available after taking time for analysis and reflection.

• *Nuclear Force Composition and Posture for Retaliation Only*—this measure would aim at structuring a nation's force posture so that it would have a secure, ample nuclear retaliatory capacity, even after sustaining a massive nuclear attack, but which would not contain destabilizing weapons, weapons that have no deterrent capacity.

This would require weapons systems whose primary requirement would be the ability to survive attack. Extreme accuracy, especially combined with multiple warheads, would be undesirable, since the ability to destroy hard targets is destabilizing, especially in a system itself vulnerable. The U.S. MX missile and the Soviet SS-18 and SS-19 are examples of types of weapons that should be eliminated. Space weapons such as antisatellite weapons and, especially, "Star Wars" defense systems are the antithesis of minimizing the nuclear role; on the contrary, they seek the ability to fight nuclearly. They should not be built.

The command and control systems would need to be as reliable as humanly possible—protected and redundant. They should be designed, and the plans made, with a goal of simplicity, not the ability to get out elaborately complex and flexible war-fighting orders while under attack, but surely to transmit minimal retaliatory directives.

The tactical weapon systems designed for retaliation only should be sharply reduced in numbers and redeployed well back from lines of contact.

Putting into effect these measures, and others that would be involved in implementing a policy of minimizing the nuclear role, would be a very large undertaking, sure to encounter ardent opposition. Recognizing that nuclear weapons are unusable will be a fundamental change in a central element of both sides' defense policies, held in one form or another for over a generation. Such a change in broad, basic concepts cannot be accomplished by experts and technicians working in secret. If the change is truly to take hold, it demands discussion, debate, argument, and understanding, in governments, the military, and the publics, nationally and internationally, with allies and opponents. And in addition to the conceptual change, there must be a broad range of military changes. These will include changes in national and alliance strategy, in plans, in training and indoctrination, in military education, in doctrinal directives, and also in the organization, equipment, and weapons of the forces themselves, both conventional and nuclear. Military concepts, military plans, military posture, and military weapons will all need reexamination and modification.

The most effective vehicle for effecting this change of concept and posture is a declaration of no-first-use. Such a declaration can give coherence and direction to the hundreds of necessary contributing actions. It must be stressed that the declaration itself, the simple words on paper, would be only the symbol, the title, of wide and fundamental change in policy and forces. It is the progressive weight of those elements of the change, and their consistency with the declared policy, that will create changed mind-sets on both sides and will govern national actions.

Some argue that a no-first-use declaration would be only declaratory policy, that the decision whether or not to use nuclear weapons will be made on the basis of perceived national interest at the moment of crisis. This argument fails to recognize the weight the no-first-use declaration would have after it was built into thinking, preparations, and military structure. While it would be operationally possible to violate the declaration and launch nuclear attacks, the weight of legitimacy, expectation, preparation, planning, and operational procedures would all be against such action.

In essence, if no-first-use is declared and effectively implemented, the nations involved will have calmly evaluated in peacetime their true individual and alliance interest and decided that nuclear war is inevitably destructive of that interest. No-first-use, then, would not leave the nuclear decision to a moment of almost intolerable stress in the heat of a deteriorating crisis. The no-first-use nations would have made that decision in advance and built it into their entire military structures.

On the U.S. side, once the no-first-use declaration had been made and absorbed into plans and forces, it would almost certainly hold during hostilities; U.S. weapons would not be released except in response to hostile use. From the American standpoint, nuclear weapons except in retaliation would have moved out of the area of legitimate weapons, and into the proscribed area along with poison gas and germ warfare.

The Soviet Union, watching the *Congressional Record,* the press, professional articles, field manuals, defense budgets, and other sources, would be able to follow U.S. and Allied conceptual thinking and observe its impact on organization, hardware, and operations. They would never be able to put absolute confidence in U.S. actions in emergency, of course, but as the evidence built up, both in words and in men and weapons, the Soviets should be won to a cautious belief that they would not be hit by nuclear weapons unless they fired them first.

Similarly, the United States will be watching the Soviet Union, to see what practical effect follows from their recent no-first-use declaration. In general, the West tries to follow Soviet strategic thought through statements by responsible political and military officials, through professional military articles in the press and military journals, through official doctrinal publications, through observing military maneuvers and exercises, and through analyzing their weapons production and their military organization. If, in the next five or six years, the United States observes that all these indicators support Soviet adherence to its no-first-use declaration, the United States, too, will be able to operate on the cautious belief, not certainty, that the Soviets do not propose to be the first to let go with nuclear weapons.

With both sides sharing that reasonable confidence, the chances would be drastically reduced, if not eliminated, of either one firing nuclear weapons preemptively, or on false information, or in panic, or on warning, or, indeed, firing at all.

Given the virulent mutual suspicions that exist and the pressures that crises and conventional hostilities would generate, arriving at a firm shared no-first-use policy will not be easy. It will be driven, however, by the fact that two-sided no-first-use would be profoundly in the interest of all involved, East and West.

There are opponents of no-first-use in the West who contend that threatening nuclear response to conventional attack—extended deterrence—should be retained as a declaratory policy, though they recognize the catastrophic futility of using nuclear weapons if the conventional attack actually happened. In a word, they advocate extended deterrence as a bluff. The argument is that conventional war is terrible itself, and that also, once joined on a major scale, it would likely lead to nuclear war; the force of nuclear deterrence must therefore be leveled against conventional war as well as nuclear war.

The critically dangerous aspect of bluffing with nuclear weapons is this. For the bluff to be effective, the bluffer has to be seen to be ready to escalate to the nuclear level, ready in his concepts, in his resolve, in his forces. To convey that conviction to the opponent, the bluffer has to be ready in reality; while a very few at the apex of government might know the readiness was a bluff, virtually the entire security organization, domestic and Allied, would be planning, training, organizing, and creating weapon programs and postures under the doctrine of nuclear war-fighting, or extended deterrence.

Extended deterrence, in effect, nuclearizes the whole system, military and governmental. In deep crisis, this readiness, these expectations, will produce enormous pressures to escalate, hard or impossible to restrain. Also, of course, the evident readiness makes the antagonist presume a nuclear response. He will consider preemption, consider firing on warning, and, certainly, stand at hair-trigger readiness in crisis. With extended deterrence in effect, either as a set policy or as a bluff, the widespread existing fear is probably valid: any hostilities would lead to nuclear war. With no-first-use convincingly in place, however, escalation to nuclear weapons would be understood throughout the military and governmental security systems to be futile, catastrophic, and not to be ordered; the nonnuclear limit would hold with high probability.

In addition, the extended deterrence bluff damages the bluffer. Threatening a nuclear response divides the peoples, within and between nations. Extended deterrence, as a bluff or not, requires the complexity of dual-purpose military forces. It discourages the building of adequate conventional forces. Bluffing would pull the nuclear rug from under forces in combat at the critical point, when conventional operations were in trouble. Bluffing, in short, harms the bluffer more than the bluffee.

Would no-first-use, largely removing the declared threat of nuclear response to conventional attack, make conventional war more probable? The nuclear threat, of course, would be reduced, and consequently that risk to the conventional attacker. Possibly, in some contingency, that might tip the scales toward conventional war. However, as the mutually suicidal nature of nuclear war becomes more and more widely understood, the effectiveness of extended deterrence inevitably erodes, in any case. The threat of suicide is not a convincing sanction. Defense against, and thus sound deterrence of, conventional attack can only be accomplished with conventional forces.

It should be noted that the measures here advocated for a policy of minimizing the role of nuclear weapons are steps the superpowers are to take individually. There is a need for discussion, argumentation, and persuasion within nations, with allies, and with opponents, but these steps do not require negotiated international agreements. No-First-Use (the Soviet Union has already announced it as policy, though implementing steps remain to be taken), No-Immediate-Response, Nuclear-Force-Posture-For-Retaliation-Only, and other implementing measures increase the security of both sides even if adopted by only one. Obviously, the effect is multiplied if both adopt and act on the policies, but even then it is not a question of negotiated treaties. The effect comes from individual, independent actions—an effect both on the nation that carries out the actions and on the opposing nation that observes the actions.

Given policies of minimizing the nuclear role in both the United States and the U.S.S.R., made effective by a range of such implementing actions, there will be a high probability that neither side will fire nuclear weapons, even during conventional hostilities.

Summary: U.S.-U.S.S.R.

In summary, as concerns the U.S.-U.S.S.R. nuclear problem, each side must recognize that all-out nuclear war would be an unimaginable catastrophe, mutually and perhaps globally suicidal. They must appreciate that each side continues to exist only with the cooperation—the restraint—of the other. The other side, then, is an opponent, an antagonist, a competitor, but not, irrevocably, an enemy, much less an inhuman monster. Each side must in the end depend on the other for life itself.

Opposing national interests and diversity of goals exist, however. These interests can be defended, on occasion, only with risk of confrontation and even war. In the nuclear age, that risk should be met, not by a great effort to "win" nuclear war, not by building a posture that tries to give hope of "controlling" nuclear war at some endurable level, but by denuclearizing the relationship as far as possible, minimizing the role of nuclear weapons in the security structures of the two countries.

This requires mutual recognition of the truth that these nuclear devices are not weapons, in the sense of tools for accomplishing human purposes; their effects are too overpowering to be proportionate to rational ends.

Nuclear weapons have no operational use. Their only function is to deter hostile use of nuclear weapons.

France and the United Kingdom

The nuclear dilemma obviously extends beyond the United States and the U.S.S.R., to all those who have nuclear weapons or may develop or obtain them, and indeed to all others as well, since everyone would be affected by nuclear warfare. What use are nuclear weapons to these other nations or organizations? What can they do with them?

The two most formidable nonsuperpower nuclear arsenals today are those of the United Kingdom and France, and each proposes large and expensive increases in the coming years. By the end of the century, if the plans are carried out, the United Kingdom will have four new TRIDENT submarines, each armed with 16 TRIDENT II missiles carrying 8–17 highly accurate warheads—perhaps 896 150-kT warheads in a reasonable loading—of which, at any time, half or three-quarters would be at sea, essentially invulnerable. France will have 592 submarine warheads in seven submarines, plus some number of SX mobile, land-based intermediate range missiles and new strategic bombers. In this posture, either country could probably destroy the Soviet Union as a functioning society, even in second strike; almost certainly the two together could do so. This buildup, therefore, changes the threat the United Kingdom and France are able to pose to a superpower from a threat to inflict heavy but less than vital damage to a mortal threat. From the opposing side, both the United Kingdom and France are vulnerable; a Soviet urban-industrial attack, first or second strike, would destroy them, and the French/U.K. buildup will surely stimulate Soviet efforts to maintain or enhance its capability against them.

The nuclear strategies of the United Kingdom and France are quite different. The United Kingdom's nuclear forces would operate under the NATO supreme commander, whose plans are tied in with the U.S. nuclear forces. In effect, U.K. and U.S. forces would function under a single plan. The United Kingdom, of course, retains the ultimate authority, in case of overriding national need, to employ its forces as it sees fit, but basically it is prepared to function within the alliance structure, providing a relatively small fraction of NATO's nuclear weaponry, and accepting that the key operational nuclear decisions will be under U.S. control.

France firmly retains nuclear independence. Its nuclear forces are to operate under the president of France. It proposes to use them where necessary to defend French vital interests, interests not precisely defined but almost certainly including French territory. Its concept is to deter conventional or nuclear aggression by being able, even in second strike, to inflict more damage than an aggressor could gain advantage. France has tactical nuclear weapons that would be used as a final warning (not, it is emphasized, as superartillery to support the conventional battle), and strategic forces that, given the relative sizes of the French and Soviet arsenals, could only be used in an anticity strategy. In brief, as far as major European war is concerned, conventional or nuclear, France has cast her lot with nuclear deterrence and suicidal retaliation.[12]

Nuclear deterrence is powerful, but, as discussed earlier for the United States and the U.S.S.R., it is unsound to rely on it to prevent all aggression, all attacks, forever. Nuclear response, meaning suicide, would be so entirely disproportionate to less than mortal threats as to be unconvincing, and therefore ineffective as a deterrent. In the end, the concept leads to absurdities. Lieutenant General Charles Fricaud-Chagnaud, respected president of the officially supported French think tank *Fondation pour les Études de la Défense Nationale,* wrote in a recent article, ". . . our [nuclear] strategy can only be an anti-city strategy; otherwise, it could mean war (*conventional, perhaps,* but *destructive and therefore unacceptable*), or servitude"[13] (emphasis supplied). What the italicized parenthetical phrase says is that since conventional war would cause much serious destruction, France would instead choose to initiate the unimaginable catastrophe of an urban-industrial nuclear exchange, which would destroy the cities, the fabric, the culture, and most of the population of the nation.

Both France and the United Kingdom are more exposed than the United States to the formidable conventional power of the Soviet Union. France lacks even the still substantial obstacle of the English Channel. Both countries, as well as other NATO members, are understandably concerned with presenting a convincing defense posture to the Warsaw Pact. The United Kingdom and, especially, France, for the time being at least, have chosen to depend in large measure on the equalizing power of the atom, at a substantial cost to their conventional power.

As in the cases of the United States and the U.S.S.R., however, depending on the nuclear crutch is dangerous, ultimately disastrous. Sooner or later, in one crisis or another, the mindsets created by maintaining physical and mental readiness to respond nuclearly to conventional attack will take control of actions and catastrophe will ensue.

For France and the United Kingdom, as for the United States and the U.S.S.R., the only reasonable role for nuclear forces is to deter hostile firing of nuclear weapons; for this function the overwhelming power of the nuclear weapon is commensurate with the challenge. The rational nuclear policy for the United Kingdom and France, as for the United States and the U.S.S.R., therefore, is to minimize the nuclear role, and especially to adopt No-First-Use. Europe can only be defended, in any meaningful sense, by conventional forces.

A critical problem exists in NATO, which could become acutely divisive. From NATO's beginning, nuclear release has been in the hands of the U.S. president, as the source of the vast bulk of the nuclear force. The president is supposed to consult the Allies before firing, if time permits. It is assumed that time will permit consultation if it is NATO that is to cross the nuclear threshold and initiate nuclear war. (It is generally accepted that *responding* to a hostile nuclear attack is an almost automatic decision that does not need consultation, and that, in any case, time would usually not permit.) An agreement to consult, however, does not yield power to decide, which remains in U.S. hands for U.S. and NATO weapons. France, as noted above, retains entire authority over French weapons.

Is this situation endurable in the long run? In Central European hostilities, can the United Kingdom or France, or, for that matter, West Germany, the Low Countries, or others, tolerate the American president's independent power, even over the expressed objections of their chiefs of state, to raise the conflict from conventional to nuclear with the almost certain result of their almost absolute destruction? Or can the United States accept the decision of the French president—or the U.K. prime minister—to initiate nuclear operations over the objections of the U.S. president in a war in which the United States is deeply engaged, when the outcome would with high probability be escalation to intercontinental nuclear exchange and catastrophe for the United States and the planet?

Almost certainly not. By one arrangement or another, the unprecedented life-and-death power of one chief of state over his allies' literal existence must be moderated. Adoption of the policy of minimizing the nuclear role, by all NATO nuclear powers, would effectively eliminate the issue. NATO would no longer face the decision of ordering first use. The Allies would have calmly evaluated in peacetime their true individual and collective interest, and decided that nuclear war is inevitably destructive of that interest. They would not leave the nuclear decision to a single authority, not responsible to most of the people involved, at a moment of almost intolerable stress in the heat of a deteriorating situation. They would have made the decision in advance, and built it into their entire military posture.

Other Nuclear Forces

Are there roles for smaller nuclear arsenals, defined, perhaps, as forces not on a scale to devastate a major country or to risk a global ecological calamity? Such forces do produce concern in and therefore leverage on opponents of the possessors. Presumably China's modest force, held under a no-first-use declaration, has some deterrent effect on the U.S.S.R., though it is not at present of a size to be decisive, and it does not appear deeply to alarm Vietnam or India. The Israeli attack on the Iraqi nuclear installation showed how powerful the Israeli reaction was to even a potential nuclear threat; one can foresee profound Israeli concern if Pakistan produces a "Moslem bomb." A number of countries feel pressures to produce or obtain weapons, for political leverage, deterrence, or even operations.

There are, however, persuasive reasons against building a nuclear force. The force and its delivery systems are an initial and a continuing major expense in human and material resources. Having a nuclear potential exposes the possessor to an increased risk of nuclear war; it automatically becomes a nuclear target for other nuclearly armed nations, and its own forces may be launched ill-advisedly, in error, in frustration, or by loss of control. For actual operations, there are few if any rational targets. During the Falklands war, some young Britons were seen with T-shirts reading "Nuke Buenos Aires," a notion that could not conceivably have commended itself to Her Majesty's Government. The appalling loss of innocent life and the physical destruction would have been insanely disproportionate to the end sought. The blast would have set off enduring hatreds in Argentina, profound antagonism and suspicions around the world even among Britain's closest allies, and deep divisions in Britain itself. Probably, among other more disastrous results, it would have meant the loss of the Falklands, as worldwide support flowed to Agentina.

Other somewhat more persuasive scenarios can be conceived, but they encounter, always, the basic reality: nuclear weapon effects are too powerful to be used for rational human purposes. Still, operationally effective or not, old enmities or deep frustrations could produce firing: of Arabs against Israel, of Iran or Iraq against the other. And a country under a fanatic leader, or a terrorist group willing to die for its cause, would not be governed by rational considerations. There is, then, some real risk of small-scale nuclear firing, with one or the other of two levels of consequences. The first would be that the limited firing, or even exchange, would stand alone, that major nuclear powers would not become engaged. Even such a limited exchange would, of course, have tragic local results. The experiences of Hiroshima and Nagasaki are examples. Further, it would rupture the political and psychological barriers against nuclear use that have been slowly built since Nagasaki; subsequent wars would be much more likely to be nuclear. It would not, however, be a global catastrophe. The targeted nation or nations would survive; aid would be available.

The other possible consequence of small-scale nuclear use is that it would trigger engagement by major nuclear powers, that they would be set off by an unidentified nuclear blast or blasts or would be led into joining hostilities between their allies or client states. Here is the risk of overwhelming disaster.

The policies that follow from the possibility of local nuclear firing include pressing nonproliferation, promoting security of weapons and weapons material to keep them out of terrorist or irresponsible hands, stressing the adverse consequences of nuclear possession and nuclear use, and advocating the minimum nuclear role policy worldwide. Against the trigger effect, the proper policy is evident: a policy of minimizing the nuclear role, especially No-Immediate-Response.

In sum, for major nuclear powers, for small nuclear powers, for nonnuclear powers, as for superpowers, the enemy is nuclear war. Nuclear weapons are too powerful, the structure and fabric of nations too fragile, the control of weapons too weak, perhaps the ecosystem too vulnerable, to use nuclear weapons operationally. Their entire role is deterring the firing of hostile nuclear weapons.

Arms Control: Old Debate, New Departures
Michael Nacht

No new significant U.S.-Soviet nuclear arms control agreement has entered into force in more than a decade. In May 1972, when the SALT (Strategic Arms Limitation Talks) I agreements were reached, they were ratified in the U.S. Senate by a vote of 88 to 2. There was a broad sense of optimism that, as President Nixon proclaimed, we were on the threshold of moving U.S.-Soviet relations from a confrontational to a cooperative basis.

Since this proclamation we have witnessed a sharp deterioration in superpower relations, triggered by the Soviet invasion of Afghanistan and the subsequent decision of President Carter to withdraw the SALT II treaty from the Senate ratification process. Although the superpower arms control negotiations resumed seriously in mid-March 1985 along a three-tiered track of strategic nuclear forces, intermediate nuclear forces, and space-based systems, neither the Geneva summit meeting between President Reagan and General Secretary Gorbachev in November 1985 nor the discussion of bold measures by these leaders at Reykjavik in October 1986 has led to agreements.

It is therefore incumbent upon those outside government to think hard about how to rejuvenate arms control and indeed to rethink what we are trying to achieve with respect to the control of nuclear weapons. It is useful in this regard first to review what have been the underlying objectives of the arms control negotiating process, and how this process has been judged by both practitioners and scholars in the field. Then, it is hoped, we shall be better positioned to offer alternatives that have the proper mixture of innovativeness and practicality to be worthy of adoption by our government.

Objectives and Perspective

It should be recalled that arms control was thought of from the beginning as a middle ground between general and complete disarmament, on the one hand, and unconstrained arms competition among potential adversaries, on the other. The former was considered utopian in a world in which sovereign states would always acquire arms to defend their national interests. The latter was judged to be a recipe for conflict in which the dynamics of the arms competition itself could exacerbate suspicions and misperceptions and lead to war. As articulated by civilian strategists in the late 1950s and early 1960s, arms control was defined as any measure that contributed to one or more of the following objectives: to reduce the likelihood of war; to reduce the damage should war occur; and to reduce the costs of preparing for war.[1] These might be termed the classical objectives of arms control.

A central assumption of those supporting these objectives was that it was vital to minimize the incentives of either superpower to strike first with nuclear weapons. If neither side had such an incentive even in a U.S.-Soviet confrontation, then "crisis stability" would be maintained. To contribute to crisis stability, arms control advocates opposed the deployment of weapons systems with high accuracy that could traverse intercontinental distances rapidly on the ground that these weapons would be "counterforce" systems that could destroy the nuclear forces of the other side. If one side deployed large numbers of these systems and their national leaders felt confident they could disarm the other, then the side with extensive counterforce capabilities would have an incentive to strike first. Moreover, the government with the vulnerable forces might expect that it would soon be struck and might therefore initiate a "preemptive" strike seeking to beat the other superpower to the nuclear draw. Weapons systems designed to target intercontinental ballistic missiles (ICBMs) based in underground silos ("countersilo weapons") were judged to be particularly destabilizing.

The other major premise of the arms control community was that, paradoxically, defenses against missile attack were undesirable. Here the reasoning went that because of inherent technological limitations neither side could develop a leakproof defense—one that destroyed virtually 100 percent of all attacking reentry vehicles. Offensive systems had simply become too sophisticated to be fully negated by antiballistic missiles (ABMs) or other defenses. But this was all to the good, since the realization by each side that it was defenseless in the face of a retaliatory attack would eliminate any incentive to strike first.

The completion of the ABM Treaty in 1972, which limited both sides to insignificant numbers of ABM interceptors, codified the notion that "assured destruction" could be inflicted by the United States and the Soviet Union on each other even after one side struck first. And this dual capability—known as mutual assured destruction (shortened to MAD by its critics)—became the hallmark of arms control supporters. These advocates sought to preserve the peace through mutual deterrence while seeking to reduce systematically the nuclear arsenals of both powers through the arms control negotiation process.

While this perspective on arms control did and still does claim many adherents, it has always suffered from an inability to take domestic and international political considerations sufficiently into account. The fact is that the weapons procurement process, including nuclear weapons acquisitions, in the United States and probably the Soviet Union as well, is determined to only a limited degree by strategic logic and judgments about crisis stability. Rather, the weapons procured reflect the outcome of complex bargaining processes within military services, between military services, and between bureaucratic alliances that cut across the executive and legislative branches and also involve active participation by a myriad of nongovernmental special interest groups.

This is the domestic reality, at least in the United States and perhaps in part in the Soviet Union as well. For diplomatic purposes weapons are deployed to make implicit political statements to adversaries and allies, in addition to their intrinsic military value. Weapons, and therefore the efforts to control them, are part of foreign policy and cannot be separated from the general tenor of international politics. Consequently those who have argued that nuclear arms control should be decoupled from other aspects of U.S.-Soviet relations have never been able to make this case stick. Soviet behavior in Afghanistan or the Kremlin's treatment of its domestic critics invariably affect American and West European attitudes toward the Soviet Union, in turn altering the domestic political base for arms control agreements. Hence, largely as a result of factors not directly related to the nuclear arms competition per se, support in the Senate for the SALT II Treaty was far weaker than it had been seven years previously for SALT I.

Henry Kissinger personified a perspective on arms control that placed it in this broader and more complex political setting. While Kissinger and President Nixon were extraordinarily well informed on the details of the nuclear balance and the arms control measures that would serve American strategic interests, they emphasized that nuclear arms control was not an end in itself but a means to a broader political purpose. Their policy of "détente" was designed to enmesh the Soviets in an intricate web of international agreements and commitments that would have the effect of mitigating the aggressiveness of Soviet foreign policy. Détente was intended to complicate Soviet decision-making processes and induce linkages between the promise of increased American economic assistance and the requirement of more cooperative Soviet international behavior. Nixon and Kissinger consistently sought to orchestrate their arms control posture to satisfy both domestic and foreign policy objectives and never restricted themselves to the literal interpretation of arms control, which remained solely within the confines of strategic logic.[2]

Throughout the 1970s, when first the Nixon-Kissinger strategy and then the Carter approach were applied to SALT, there was always a minority view largely hostile to both perspectives. The history of the 1970s strengthened this viewpoint until, with the election of Ronald Reagan as president in 1980, it came to dominate official American policy.

This perspective emphasizes the deleterious "lulling effects" on American national security of arms control negotiations and agreements and in large measure rejects or is at least deeply skeptical of each of the assumptions cited above. In terms of strategic calculus, this school has consistently emphasized that what preserves the nuclear peace is a credible nuclear deterrent, and that to be credible U.S. forces must be so configured as to be able to engage in limited and/or sustained nuclear warfare. These convictions, embraced earlier in Secretary of Defense James Schlesinger's declaratory policy of "limited nuclear options" and by Secretary of Defense Harold Brown's proclamations of a "countervailing strategy," were taken even further under the Reagan administration.

Proponents of this viewpoint argue that in a world of increasingly accurate delivery systems, it is essential for the United

States to deploy forces capable of targeting the full array of Soviet forces plus command and control centers. Not only, therefore, do they reject the arms controllers' concerns for crisis stability. They are also highly critical of the premises upon which the ABM Treaty was supported, asserting that reliance on assured destruction is both a noncredible and a dangerous policy. They believe that moving toward more effective defenses is the only way to extricate ourselves from the nuclear sword of Damocles that hangs over us.

Given the totalitarian nature of the Soviet political system, advocates of the "lulling" school of thought reject the contention that arms control can be used as a means toward moderation of Soviet foreign policy. They point to the major strides taken by the Soviets despite the SALT regime both in the buildup of their nuclear forces and in aggressiveness in Sub-Saharan Africa and other parts of the Third World. Both are seen as evidence that the Soviet leadership can totally insulate its foreign and military policies from the arms control process. But, it is argued, the pluralistic American system lulls itself into a false sense of security by equating arms control with national safety. The extreme view sees arms control, therefore, as a dangerous diplomatic narcotic whose net effect is to weaken American defenses and embolden Soviet leaders.

Every key element of the Reagan administration's nuclear force modernization and arms control program—the acceleration of the deployment schedule of countersilo weapons; the support for funds for antisatellite (ASAT) weapons; declaratory support and budgetary increases for a civil defense program; the strategic defense initiative (SDI); the desire to eliminate perceived Soviet advantages in missile throw-weight and other quantitative measures of the nuclear arsenal; and an initial slow approach in arms control negotiations—all reflect a rejection of earlier American interpretations of arms control. It is an approach that, despite occasional rhetorical shifts, has been carried forward during President Reagan's second term in the White House.[3]

To the extent that bipartisanship once prevailed in U.S. arms control policy, it has long since disappeared. While public opinion polls continue to indicate broad support for reaching new arms control agreements with the Soviets, the same polls suggest a strong distrust of the Russians and the need to continue to repair American defenses (albeit, now with reduced budget-

ary increases in the wake of the passage of the Gramm-
Rudman-Hollings Balanced Budget Amendment).[4] Given the
asymmetries between U.S. and Soviet nuclear forces (for example, roughly 75% of the Soviet megatonnage resides in their
fixed, land-based missiles, whereas somewhat less than 30% of
U.S. megatonnage is in American ICBMs), the inability to reach
a common understanding as to research and development
activities associated with strategic defense that would be permissible under the ABM Treaty, and a Soviet decision-making
process that remains characterized by conservatism and ineffi-
ciencies, the outlook for the completion of new meaningful superpower arms control agreements cannot be judged to be
great.

Enduring Challenges

In assessing the prospects for arms control, a number of enduring issues must be faced: (1) How can the pace of diplomatic negotiations match the technological momentum that
stimulates the weapons acquisition process? (2) Can qualitative
as well as quantitative nuclear arms control be achieved and, if
so, how? (3) Given the great political significance placed on the
ability to verify Soviet compliance of arms control agreements,
how should verification fit into American arms control strategy? (4) Beyond bilateral negotiations, are there other useful
approaches, such as mutual example and reciprocal actions, by
which meaningful arms limitations can be achieved? (5) There
are special problems of force deployment, declaratory policy,
and arms control posture associated with our European allies.
How shall these be addressed? (6) Are there ways to adjust the
American domestic constraints on arms control to enhance national security as well as the prospects for agreement? The balance of this paper will briefly examine the first three issues and
the companion paper by Jane Sharp will address the final three.

The Negotiations Process
The historical record demonstrates that the pace of arms control negotiations has become more ponderous as the issues have
grown increasingly complex. The SALT I accords took almost
three years to negotiate and required last-minute concessions
by an American president running for reelection in order for
agreement to be reached. The SALT II Treaty, after many fits

and starts, was not signed till seven years later and never ratified by the United States. In the meantime research and development processes produced multiple independently targetable reentry vehicles (MIRVs), the air-breathing cruise missile, antisatellite systems, and other advances that complicate enormously the measurement of the nuclear balance and efforts to control force levels.

It must be recognized, however, that these processes of negotiation and technological development are not carried out fully independently of each other. Indeed it has been the practice of each American administration, in defending arms control before the Senate, to assert that the particular agreement under consideration in no way hampers the plans for deployment of the next generation of nuclear weapons! Therefore it is simplistic to see the issue as one of negotiations in slow motion consistently overtaken by rapid technological advance. Rather, the very negotiating positions placed on the table with the Soviets are the product of intense interagency bargaining that takes into account the anticipated output of the research and development process. In this bargaining the most advanced systems are, almost always, protected from the arms control process. This was true in the case of MIRVs in SALT I and cruise missiles in the Vladivostok negotiations in the early stages of SALT II, and is evident in the Reagan administration's position on strategic defenses in the negotiations that began in March 1985.

Furthermore a close reading of the arms control record indicates that it would be naive to conclude that either the United States or the Soviet Union was primarily motivated by the desire to effectuate a more stable strategic balance. While this objective was surely a high priority of some participants, the dominant military motivation for arms control has been to gain unilateral advantage or to prevent the other side from attaining advantages it would have acquired in the absence of agreement. Through the 1970s, in fact, the more rapid pace of ongoing Soviet nuclear deployments placed the United States at a distinct negotiating disadvantage. For example, with respect to the numerically unequal offensive force levels stipulated in the SALT I Interim Agreement, the Nixon administration defended them on the ground that without agreement, the numerical disparities in favor of the Soviets would have been even greater. Similar arguments were used in SALT II to explain the heavy missile disparity (308 Soviet heavy missiles permitted, compared with none for the United States).

It would appear that the Soviets have approached arms control in a similar fashion. In retrospect, for example, the Soviet negotiating position over permissible ICBM silo dimensions during SALT I was designed to facilitate the deployment of the next generation of ICBMs then in the stage of advanced engineering development. And indeed a few former Soviet officials now living in the West who were familiar with the evolution of the Kremlin's arms control negotiating positions have asserted that Soviet diplomacy at the bargaining table was never permitted to interfere with the decisions already taken by the Defense Council to deploy major nuclear weapons systems. A stereotypical view held by some arms control advocates of outgunned diplomats facing a losing battle in trying to keep pace with the momentum of technological advance does not therefore square with the facts. While it is surely the case that the march of technology does oftentimes complicate the life of the negotiator, the political and military leadership of both superpowers has consistently used the arms control process in ways compatible with their own force modernization plans and programs.

Numbers or Quality?

With respect to qualitative versus quantitative constraints in arms control, it has long been clear that the former is more significant, but more elusive, than the latter. The United States agreed in SALT I to an inferior number of ICBM and submarine-launched ballistic missile (SLBM) launchers in part because of its advantage in MIRV technology and warhead accuracy. Subsequently, of course, these same capabilities acquired by the Soviets became the essential problem concerning ICBM vulnerability, generating in turn the acrimonious and continuing debate on the disposition of the MX missile.

For many years the United States eschewed the development of antisatellite (ASAT) weapons, only to be stimulated by the testing of a crude, low-altitude Soviet device. A 1977 U.S. proposal for ASAT negotiations was cooly received by the Soviets. Subsequently, after a few preliminary rounds were held, the negotiations were terminated by the United States following the Soviet invasion of Afghanistan. More recently, with a major U.S. ASAT program now being funded, it is the Soviets who have sought to convene such negotiations, only to be greeted by a relatively unenthusiastic American response.

In short, major qualitative improvements have been jealously guarded by each superpower as long as it thought it retained a real or potential advantage. Only when its advantage failed to materialize did there develop a serious interest in constraining the weapons development through negotiated agreement. And given the large number of warheads already deployed by the United States and the U.S.S.R. (in excess of 60,000), it is surely qualitative rather than quantitative improvements in the forces that have the potential to destabilize the nuclear balance and provide first-strike incentives. Since these qualitative improvements would permit the armed forces to wage war more effectively—and this, after all, is their mission if called upon to do so—it is precisely these systems that are most difficult to negotiate away.

Verification

A third critical issue is the question of verifying Soviet compliance with arms control agreements, a largely asymmetric concern the Soviets have rarely raised in the negotiating process. Presumably the openness of American society and the magnitude of the Soviet intelligence-gathering effort provide sufficient confidence to the Politburo of their ability to verify American compliance. In the American politial process, however, Soviet compliance is a major issue.

Apart from routine ongoing efforts by the U.S. intelligence community to monitor Soviet military behavior irrespective of the status of arms control agreements, the verification process involves four basic steps:

a. collecting data on the status of Soviet programs,

b. interpreting the data in the light of treaty obligations,

c. determining with a specified level of confidence Soviet compliance with existing treaties, and

d. choosing how to proceed if the Soviets are judged to have violated an agreement.

Controversy surrounds every step. Because of the ambiguous language of certain provisions of existing agreements and the inherent ambiguity in assessing Soviet behavior, honest observers can differ as to whether treaty violations have been committed. Moreover, the verification process is itself not immune to political pressure on the part of individuals and institutions.

If Soviet violations are indeed confirmed, several avenues then need to be explored. If the transgression is not judged to be militarily significant—itself a contentious judgment—it would in any event claim the attention of senior-level government officials. If, however, the violation was judged to be significant, several options are available: raise the issue formally in the Standing Consultative Commission (SCC), which was established at the time of SALT I expressly to hear such grievances; raise the issue through other diplomatic channels, such as directly with the Soviet ambassador to the United States, or by the U.S. ambassador in Moscow with officials in the Soviet Foreign Ministry; leak it to the press and have the issue enter the American public debate "unofficially"; or go public through formal statements by the president or other high-level U.S. officials.

At present there is a range of outstanding issues concerning Soviet compliance with both the SALT I and SALT II agreements (note that while SALT II never legally entered into force, both the United States and the Soviet Union mostly abided by its provisions beginning in 1979—until the U.S. said in 1986 it would no longer consider it binding). Particularly disturbing are allegations that the Soviets are constructing a large phased-array radar at Krasnoyarsk in Central Asia that would almost certainly violate the ABM Treaty.[5] According to a report submitted by the Reagan Administration to Congress in January 1984,

The Soviet Union is violating the Geneva Protocol on Chemical Weapons, the Biological Weapons Convention, the Helsinki Final Act, and two provisions of SALT II: telemetry encryption and a rule concerning ICBM modernization. In addition, we have determined that the Soviet Union has almost certainly violated the ABM Treaty, probably violated the SALT II limits on new types of weapons and deployment of intercontinental missiles and is likely to have violated the nuclear testing yield limit of the Threshold Test Ban Treaty.[6] Of course we have not ratified either SALT II or the test ban.

Some of these claims are contentious. However, in this author's judgment, there is a widespread belief in the expert community that the building of the Krasnoyarsk radar is a definite violation of the ABM Treaty and that the deployment of the

Soviet SS-25 and the encryption of telemetry data of missile flight tests are indeed violations of the SALT II Treaty.

Although neither SALT II nor the Threshold Test Ban Treaty has been ratified by the U.S. Senate, they are part of the existing arms control regime that is at the core of present U.S.-Soviet relations. With the publication of more detailed evidence supporting these claims, it may become increasingly difficult to sustain American political support for further arms control negotiations. Critics of the administration will claim that this is precisely the intent behind such publication. The accumulation of numerous confirmed incidents of questionable Soviet behavior places even the most ardent supporters of arms control in a precarious situation.

If the issues are raised at the SCC and resolved satisfactorily to all parties, no harm is done. But since this has not been the case in several instances—it has been alleged by a high-level unattributable source that the Krasnoyarsk issue has been raised by the United States at 77 meetings of the SCC since 1983 without resolution—Washington has had the choice of suppressing the information, in which case it would be accused of being a witting accomplice to Soviet transgressions, or revealing the violations and running the risk of doing further damage to U.S.-Soviet relations. There is no simple escape from these difficult choices. The ease of the verification task, it should be emphasized, is directly correlated to the clarity of the treaty language specifying what behavior is permissible. Vague and complex language is the enemy of effective verification.

Arms Control Options

Given this evolution of the negotiating experience and the particular challenges raised by the verification issue, what options for arms control are realistically available? Several have been publicly debated, and a few additional proposals are worthy of consideration.

A Nuclear Freeze

This proposal commanded widespread public attention and support in 1982–1983 and was endorsed by presidential candidate Walter F. Mondale in the 1984 presidential election. It has been most often proposed as a mutual and verifiable ban on the production, testing, and deployment of all new missiles and aircraft that have nuclear weapons as their principal or sole payload. Advocates of the freeze see it as putting a stop to the force modernization process, which they regard as the engine that drives the arms race. Some advocates go so far as to see the freeze as the first step toward not only a denuclearized world, but one in which the role of force in international politics is no longer an acceptable mode of national conduct.

There are three principal objections to the freeze. The first is that important elements of it, particularly with respect to production, cannot be verified with high confidence. This is a contentious assertion on which knowledgeable individuals are divided. There is little doubt that full-range testing of ballistic missiles can be adequately verified. One could adopt counting rules so that the number of warheads observed being tested on a missile would count as the number of deployed warheads for all missiles of this type. The locations of the production of fissionable material are also identifiable, although the output of these facilities may not be precisely determinable. But the numbers and locations of cruise missiles, especially sea-launched cruise missiles, cannot be verified with great confidence. Nor can weapons system component and subcomponent testing be easily detected.

A second objection is that the proposed freeze would "freeze" several disparities (especially ICBM hard-target kill capabilities) that favor the Soviet Union. And a third objection is that important nonnuclear capabilities (particularly antisubmarine warfare systems) would remain unconstrained, and possibly promote instability in a situation where the number of ballistic missile submarines was frozen.

Several years of widespread public support for the freeze was not translatable into sufficient congressional support to produce legislation. Nor has there been any alteration in the Reagan administration's opposition to the proposal.

Build-Down

In the spring of 1984 the Reagan administration, following congressional pressure, introduced at negotiations in Geneva a "build-down" formula, which was greeted coolly by the chief Soviet negotiator. The build-down formula has several complex variations, but the basic concept is that for each new nuclear warhead or delivery vehicle introduced into the arsenals of the superpowers, at least twice as many existing systems would have to be discarded. Therefore, while force modernization would continue, the number of deployed forces would decline.

The principal problems with this proposal are, first, that it would not constrain the mix of forces, so that the net result could be the introduction of more "destabilizing" counterforce weapons as the number of inaccurate obsolescent weapons is reduced; and second, it does not lend to the arms competition the element of predictability, which is a major confidence-building goal of the arms control process. Rather, the build-down formula would permit the nuclear force modernization process to continue in ways designed to threaten the retaliatory forces of each superpower. Political liberals have been particularly opposed to this concept on the grounds that it would be a stimulus to the arms race under the guise of arms control.

"Midgetman"

The President's Commission on Strategic Forces—the so called "Scowcroft Commission"—recommended in January 1983 that serious research and development commence on a single-warhead missile commonly known as Midgetman. The rationale behind this proposal is that missiles with multiple independently targetable reentry vehicles (MIRVs) are the principal source of instability: they place a premium on attacking first, since an attacker can use a small percentage of its MIRVed missiles to destroy a large percentage of the adversary's missiles. Deploying single-warhead missiles, it is argued, would be a step in the right direction. A world of only single-warhead missiles would be more stable because the attacker would be committing mutual disarmament if it needed to use the same number of missiles to destroy opposing missiles. Put another way, reducing the warhead-to-missile ratio of the forces contributes to stability. The attractiveness of this proposal, therefore, hinges on the likelihood of being able to move to a world without MIRVs—a highly desirable objective. (Since President Reagan publicly declared in the spring of 1986 that the United States would no longer be bound by the SALT II Treaty, questions of the permissibility of Midgetman deployment under the terms of the treaty are presumably moot.)

If Midgetman merely supplements rather than replaces existing systems—and there have now been proposals introduced to place MIRVs on Midgetman missiles—it will serve no arms control purpose.

"No-First-Use" Pledge

Besides proposals to constrain or reduce nuclear force deployments, there have been calls for the United States to pledge, as the Soviet Union has already, not to be the first to use nuclear weapons. Proponents have argued that this makes sense because NATO has never developed any clear strategy for using nuclear weapons that would not lead to the likely destruction of much of Western Europe. The proposal is also seen as a stimulus for our European allies to build up their conventional forces on the premise that they would no longer be able to rely upon U.S. nuclear retaliation in the event of a Soviet conventional attack in central Europe. Opponents of the idea claim it would undermine alliance cohesion and reduce uncertainty for Soviet military planners. They argue that there is no evidence to suggest that it would produce the desired buildup of Western conventional forces.

The former Allied Commander in Europe (SACEUR), General Bernard Rogers, has publicly supported the idea of "no early first use" of nuclear weapons and has urged NATO to acquire a capability to strike deeply into Warsaw Pact territory with conventional weapons to destroy second-echelon pact forces. Both proposals are designed to reduce NATO's reliance on nuclear weapon use in the early stages of a conflict in Europe. But, as of this writing, there is no evidence to suggest that the United States is moving in the direction of formally endorsing the "no first use" pledge.

Comprehensive Test Ban Treaty

There has long been support to conclude a comprehensive nuclear test ban treaty (CTBT), especially since the Limited Test Ban Treaty was signed and ratified in 1963. The basis for support of the CTBT is that prohibiting all testing would diminish the confidence of war planners in the reliability of their nuclear weapon systems, presumably reducing the likelihood of their use. (Note, however, that the atomic bomb dropped at Hiroshima in August 1945 was of an untested design!)

Arguments against a treaty, which have proved to be very durable for more than two decades, are principally three: a CTBT cannot be verified at low weapon yields (indeed the Threshold Nuclear Test Ban Treaty, which was signed in 1974 but never ratified, specifies a limit of underground tests to 150 KT—kilotons—that has probably been exceeded by the Soviets); a CTBT would reduce the reliability of existing weapon stockpiles, yet high reliability is vital to maintain deterrence and retaliate effectively should deterrence fail; moreover, it is claimed, a CTBT would drive away qualified scientific and engineering personnel from work on nuclear weapon systems research and development—a necessary capability to be maintained to guard against a sudden Soviet "breakout" of the agreement. As with many of the proposals already cited, there is no prospect at present that such a treaty will be put forward by the Reagan administration for serious negotiation with the Soviets.

The Utilization of Space

To prevent the deployment of weapon systems that would be able to attack early warning and communication satellites would seem to be in the interest of both superpowers. A ban on ground-based and space-based antisatellite (ASAT) weapons, together with the prohibition of the deployment of weapon systems of any kind in space, would be a highly significant arms control achievement. (Note that the Outer Space Treaty presently prohibits the deployment of nuclear weapons in space.) The Reagan administration has shown little interest in these proposals, in part because it claims that they are not verifiable. More important, though, they cut against the president's Strategic Defense Initiative (SDI), which has as its stated goal to render nuclear weapons "impotent and obsolete."

In the vigorous public debate on the merits of SDI that has surfaced since President Reagan's reelection, several particularly salient points have emerged. First, the Soviet Union has as its highest priority the cessation of a U.S. research and development program whose aim would be to perfect effective defenses for both missile silos and population centers against a major Soviet ICBM and submarine-launched ballistic missile (SLBM) attack. Second, the Reagan administration is adamant about proceeding with research in strategic defense and gained congressional approval to provide in excess of $3 billion for FY (federal year) 1987 to support such efforts. Third, the administration claims knowledge of a significant Soviet program to investigate strategic defenses and is leery that any prohibition of such research could be verified. Fourth, space-based and defensive systems are the subject of one of the three U.S.-Soviet arms control negotiations resumed in Geneva in 1985, and it was failure to reach mutual agreement on permissible SDI activities that led to a breakdown in the negotiations at Reykjavik. It is apparent that a fundamental premise of the U.S. position is confidence in American superiority in the relevant technologies for both space and defensive applications and a deep reluctance to negotiate this advantage away at the bargaining table.

Conclusions

On balance, it would seem that there are certain opportunities for arms control if the following conditions are met. These observations could serve as useful guidelines for any administration's approach to negotiated nuclear arms control with the Soviet Union—assuming, that is, that such agreements genuinely represent a high priority for leaders in both Washington and Moscow.

• There must be a clear presidential commitment to arms control and strong presidential leadership to guide the interagency negotiating process, the international negotiations, and the politics of ratification.

• Arms control must be coupled with force modernization, and sold to the Congress and to the American public as *part of national strategy.* Arms control alone cannot carry the weight of being either synonymous with or an alternative to a comprehensive national security policy.

• Simplicity is highly desirable in any negotiated agreement. The more complex the document, the more easily opponents can identify one element upon which to base their opposition. The greater the complexity, the more difficult it is to sustain support for the agreement in American politics.

• Numbers of weapon systems or warheads tell us little about stability. What is crucial is the relative vulnerability of each side's strategic forces to a sudden, disarming attack. The aim of arms control should be to lessen vulnerabilities, not to reduce numbers per se.

• Related to the objective of reduced vulnerability are the goals of transparency and warning. Any steps taken to increase the predictability of force deployments or to increase warning time to strengthen decision-making processes in crises are highly desirable and should be thought of as an integral part of arms control.

• Exclusionary agreements—the Outer Space Treaty, the Sea Bed Treaty, the Antarctic Treaty—have been successfully negotiated in the past. It is easier to preclude weapons deployments from a region where they have never been than to regulate those that are already in place. To deny the militarization of outer space, therefore, has at least some encouraging precedents, including the Outer Space Treaty already in force.

• Arms control agreements need not be limited to the imposition of symmetrical constraints. If the United States finds that Soviet heavy ICBMs are highly objectionable whereas the Soviet Union is disturbed by U.S. cruise missile deployments, there is nothing in principle to block a one-for-one asymmetrical agreement as long as the net vulnerabilities of both sets of forces are reduced.

• We must be realistic about what arms control can achieve. Given the deep political, economic, and philosophical divisions between the superpowers, the arms race is more a symptom than a cause of the strategic competition. At best, arms control agreements would constrain, but not transform, this competition.

At the Reykjavik summit, prior to the breakdown over the status of SDI, agreements were apparently reached to reduce to zero the number of U.S. and Soviet intermediate nuclear forces in Europe and, over a ten-year period, to eliminate all ballistic missiles on both sides. It is too soon to say whether such far-reaching proposals can in fact now be negotiated into ratified agreements. If not, more modest achievements, such as those cited above, are still worthy of exploration. A third choice—offensive and defensive deployments by both powers wholly unconstrained by mutual agreement—is the least desirable alternative.

Arms Control: Alliance Cohesion and Extended Deterrence
Jane M. O. Sharp

Arms control is the process whereby potential adversaries seek to limit their military forces by international agreement so as to reduce the risk of war, to reduce the extent of damage should war occur, and to reduce the cost of preparing for war.

In an ideal world, arms control would be an integral part of prudent defense planning. Governments would buy only the forces necessary to defend against external threats and maintain internal order, and no state would frighten its neighbors with either menacing rhetoric or bellicose military postures. In practice, however, both the Soviet Union and the United States espouse offensive nuclear war-fighting doctrines and bristle with provocative hardware. Moreover, post-1945 efforts to curb Soviet-American competition in nuclear weaponry have not begun to keep pace with the development and acquisition of ever more sophisticated and destructive armaments.

In order to conclude an arms control agreement with the Soviet Union, the United States must pursue at least three sets of negotiations: the main bilateral forum with the Soviets, another set of discussions with the Western allies and, often the most difficult of all, the intragovernmental bargaining in Washington necessary both to formulate its initial proposals and to ratify any agreements signed by the executive branch.

Recurring problems constrain progress at each of the three levels. Agreement with Moscow is hampered by contrasts in Soviet and American styles of negotiation and decision making, by different security needs, by different perceptions of what constitutes equity and equal security, and by deep-seated historical suspicion. Consensus is difficult to reach in NATO because of both a nuclear hierarchy in the alliance and the perceived dependence of the nonnuclear European countries on an

American nuclear security guarantee. In the United States, arms control policymaking is hostage to special interest groups in the Department of Defense, to weapons contractors, to interservice rivalries, to the vagaries of the American electoral cycle, and to the constitutional requirements of treaty making.

Coping with all these obstacles and aligning the optimal conditions to achieve agreement is a formidable task, since correcting one set of problems often exacerbates others. Meeting the requirements for agreement between the two superpowers, for example, often undermines cohesion in NATO. Expanding the dialogue—into either an interalliance forum like the NATO-Warsaw Pact negotiations on Mutual and Balanced Force Reductions in Vienna (MBFR) or a larger multilateral gathering like the Conference on Security and Cooperation in Europe (CSCE)—will improve alliance input but will surely be more cumbersome and may be at the expense of early agreement and more effective limitations.

Finally, in the domestic arena, steps taken by the executive branch to buy the support of the military establishment for a particular treaty may be at the expense of wider public support for arms control. Compensation for limits imposed on one category of weapons may come in the form of side payments on some other pet project of the service chiefs that will not only generate Soviet countermeasures but also divert resources from the social welfare budget. The public constituency for SALT II was seriously undermined, for example, by President Carter's request for increased spending on strategic systems, most particularly for the MX missile, and by his acquiescing in the Joint Chiefs' request not to press for a comprehensive test ban, steps that—ironically—were designed to broaden the base of support for the treaty.

Successful arms control seems to elude governments across the political spectrum, from ideological conservatives to liberal democrats. At this writing the Reagan administration has not signed a single agreement with the Soviets to limit military forces; but neither was the Carter administration able to pursue any agreements to ratification. And even those treaties concluded by earlier administrations did little more than codify some aspect of the status quo and rarely cut into the existing arsenals of any power. At worst, they appear to have stimulated competitive force-matching in the elusive search for balanced agreements. The most dramatic reductions have always been unilateral measures taken when the forces in question became redundant.

Thus, in order to control nuclear weapons, we must obviously go beyond traditional arms control and reassess our foreign and defense policy needs; to examine critically the purposes these forces are intended to serve, the vital interests they are supposed to defend, and the threats they are supposed to deter. This paper tackles the specific problem of trying to reconcile nuclear arms control with alliance cohesion and extended deterrence, i.e., the capability to deter a Soviet attack on our West European allies. How can the United States design its forces and conduct its arms control diplomacy in ways that do not undermine the security of either its NATO allies or its Warsaw Pact adversaries?

NATO's Nuclear Arms Control Dilemma

All military alliances suffer a common security dilemma, namely, the tensions induced by the risks of being abandoned by one's allies in a crisis and the risks of being entrapped in a conflict not of one's own choosing.[1] NATO's nuclear hierarchy, in which there are seven different classes of states with respect to their nuclear rights and obligations, exacerbates this dilemma.[2] The West European allies oscillate between two contradictory fears: on the one hand that the United States will not be willing to carry out its threat of nuclear retaliation to a non-nuclear Warsaw Pact attack, because of the risk of a Soviet counterstrike on the American homeland, and on the other, that the United States might resort to nuclear weapons too soon, try to limit nuclear warfare to Europe and incinerate the continent in the process.[3]

These fears are also reflected in West European anxieties about bilateral U.S.-U.S.S.R. arms control negotiations. The smaller NATO countries swing from anxiety that a superpower agreement will discriminate against the security interests of Western Europe, to fear that the Soviet Union and the United States will engage in an unbridled nuclear arms competition. Thus, many Europeans resented the Non-Proliferation Treaty, which restricted the nuclear weapons club to those five states that had already tested nuclear explosions by 1967, and established a highly discriminatory regime with respect to inspection of civilian nuclear power facilities.

Anxieties about abandonment were evident in European complaints that the bilateral Agreement on the Prevention of Nuclear War—signed by the two superpowers in 1973—implied that the United States was more interested in Soviet-American arms control than in its security commitment to NATO. In the late 1970s West German critics of SALT II complained that the agreement limited intercontinental-range missiles, which threatened the American homeland, while leaving unconstrained medium-range strategic missiles and bombers, which threatened Western Europe—anxieties that generated NATO's double-track decision to deploy new American missiles in western Europe.[4] Predictably—if paradoxically—West European leaders were also apprehensive in the mid-1980s when President Reagan and General Secretary Gorbachev discussed proposals for zero INF in Europe. Such an agreement would work to remove the Soviet SS-20 threat to the NATO countries but it would also remove the American cruise and Pershing II missiles that NATO leaders had worked so hard to justify a few years earlier.

The Abandonment-Entrapment Dilemma

The dependent European allies seem to experience cycles of anxiety about American leadership, which typically have five stages. Stage I represents the loss of confidence in Washington, which can be triggered by economic, political, or military anxieties. Problems can arise, for example, when the United States appears to export inflation, becomes enamoured of repressive right-wing military regimes in the Third World, engages in extra-NATO military activities that could trigger conflict in Europe, and proposes weapons programs like the Sentinel and Safeguard antiballistic missile systems in the 1960s and 1970s and the current Strategic Defense Initiative, which suggest a Fortress America approach to defense planning.[5] Particularly difficult problems to deal with are recurrent European anxieties that Soviet-American arms control negotiations are being conducted at the expense of NATO defense interests.

In stage II allies seek reassurance from Washington, and, in particular, look for signs of a renewed commitment to defend the political and territorial integrity of Western Europe. These anxieties are best dealt with in political currency. A good example was the Nuclear Planning Group, which Defense Secretary Robert McNamara established in the late 1960s to reassure Europeans troubled by a combination of nuclear worries, including the cancellation of the MLF (multilateral force) nuclear control sharing scheme and the discriminatory aspects of the Non-Proliferation Treaty.

More often, however, the cycle moves to stage III, in which the response from Washington comes in the form of the latest nuclear hardware, raising tensions and complicating arms control efforts between East and West. This then triggers stage IV, in which fear of entrapment takes over from fear of abandonment as Europeans protest the new cold war, excessive reliance on NATO's nuclear weapons, and the new risks of nuclear holocaust. In stage V, Europeans encourage a new Soviet-American rapprochement—in particular, a return to serious arms control negotiations. If the ensuing détente generates more bilateral agreements, these may trigger a new round of European fears of abandonment.

To the extent that these cycles of anxiety are attributed to overreliance on American nuclear weapons, one obvious remedy is for NATO to adopt a defense policy that relies less on the nuclear, and more on the nonnuclear, components of NATO's military force posture. This shift was indeed attempted on a number of occasions. The results were only partially successful, however, since the impetus for change usually came from the United States and was perceived by the Europeans as yet another manifestation of the lack of American commitment to the alliance, thereby becoming part of the problem rather than the solution.

Previous Efforts to Reduce NATO's Reliance on Nuclear Weapons

In the late 1950s and the early 1960s, the ability to deter a Warsaw Pact attack against Western Europe was thought to rest on the threat of massive retaliation with American nuclear weapons in response to any kind of Soviet military thrust into NATO territory. American defense analysts, notably at the RAND Corporation, questioned the rationality of this all-or-nothing policy in the late 1950s, but it was not until the late 1960s that Defense Secretary Robert S. McNamara managed to persuade NATO governments to endorse a range of less cataclysmic options.[6]

The essence of the new policy, designated "flexible response," was to respond "appropriately" to whatever level of aggression might be inflicted by an adversary. Thus, while the threat to launch intercontinental-range strategic nuclear weapons on Soviet cities might be appropriate to deter Soviet strikes on the cities of the United States, it was now deemed implausible to deter lesser acts of aggression, such as the further encroachment on West Berlin. To deter low-level threats to NATO, McNamara argued, the alliance should be capable of a range of military options, from nonnuclear, through limited nuclear, all the way up to a massive strategic response.

The European response to the proposed change was cool at best. French and British officials objected to McNamara's assertion that a vital attribute of deterrence was central American control of all NATO's nuclear assets, which implied that small, independent nuclear arsenals were both dangerous and redundant. In Bonn, NATO's threat of early and massive nuclear use was deemed the best deterrent to Soviet adventures, and West German officials were apprehensive about a policy that seemed to reduce the risks of aggression for the Warsaw Pact armies. Most European officials worried about Washington's apparent reluctance to risk American security on behalf of Western Europe and, especially, about a policy that required larger investments in conventional military forces.

French opposition was the most vociferous, and only after General de Gaulle withdrew French forces from the integrated NATO command, and pushed NATO headquarters out of France, did the other 14 governments in the integrated command structure endorse the document M/14/3 approving flexible response. This policy was a conscious compromise from the start, with no clear transatlantic consensus on what military action the policy prescribes should deterrence fail.[7] Robert McNamara's goal appeared to be to keep the nuclear threshold high, the firebreak between nuclear and conventional weapons firm, and the conventional phase of any conflict as long as possible, thereby putting the onus of nuclear escalation onto the adversary. Insofar as this kind of thinking envisages a prolonged conflict on European soil it is anathema to West European—especially West German—officials. They prefer to threaten the Soviets with the shortest possible conventional pause and the earliest nuclear use—optimally, of a strategic American attack on the Soviet Union—and to argue for military forces capable of controlling every rung in a hypothetical ladder of escalation.[8]

As long as NATO doctrine is discussed in vague terms these different perspectives do not seriously threaten alliance cohesion, but when NATO reformers try to refine flexible response and rationalize forces for specific operations, intra-NATO tensions tend to increase.[9] Thus in early 1982 when Robert McNamara and three other former government officials spelled out the irrationality of initiating the use of nuclear weapons under conditions of Soviet-American strategic parity, and advocated an explicit doctrine of no-first-use, West German officials responded predictably with alarm.[10]

In both his 1960s version of flexible response and his 1980s advocacy of no-first-use, McNamara urged stronger conventional forces for NATO and less reliance on European owned and European-based nuclear weapons. By contrast, most European officials who oppose no-first-use, while not necessarily adverse to cutting back stockpiles of vulnerable short-range battlefield systems, tend to support the modernization of NATO's intermediate-range nuclear forces (INF)—in order to maintain "escalation dominance"[11]—and oppose the buildup of conventional forces for a long war.

European governments' anxieties about no-first-use in the 1980s parallel official anxieties about flexible response in the 1960s: first, an unduly pessimistic view of the East-West balance of conventional forces; second, and flowing from the first, reluctance to allocate funds to improve nonnuclear forces because the task not only seems so enormous, but also suggests a willingness to contemplate a long conventional war; third, apprehension about American resolve to use force in defense of western Europe if it risks a retaliatory Soviet strike on the American homeland; and fourth, apprehension about the risks of tampering with anything as fundamental as alliance military doctrine.[12]

While not yet ready to accept no-first-use, and standing firm on the deployment of new intermediate-range nuclear missiles, NATO leaders nevertheless reached a consensus, in reaction to widespread protest against the double-track INF decision, that NATO must rely less on nuclear weapons. This was reflected in the NATO Shift Study undertaken at the instigation of the Dutch government, which resulted in the withdrawal of 1,000 warheads in connection with the December 1979 "double-track" decision to modernize NATO's intermediate-range nuclear forces, and the decision at Montebello in October 1983 to withdraw another 1,400. In addition, for each new INF warhead introduced in accordance with the December 1979 double-track decision, one old warhead will be removed. This still leaves some 4,600 U.S. nuclear warheads in Western Europe, and many NATO officials would like to remove more, especially those designated for nuclear artillery or other short-range, short-reaction-time, battlefield systems. Proposals to change NATO's flexible response doctrine to one of no-first-use continue to meet strong official opposition, however, and the issue will need to be thoroughly debated, particularly in West Germany, before any change can be expected.

More useful than a formal no-first-use declaration would be acceleration of the current trend toward a revised posture that implies no-early-use or very-unlikely-use by removing from Western Europe all nuclear battlefield systems, and eventually all land-based nuclear forces. Retaining the option of first-use of U.S. centrally or sea-based strategic systems would still be a powerful deterrent to Soviet military moves in a crisis. Such a posture would be less likely to generate European fears of abandonment than a formal renunciation of first use. Yet removing the provocative and vulnerable "use-them-or-lose-them" systems should also ease any fear of entrapment caused by the prospect of too-early use.

Reassessing the Requirements for Extended Deterrence

Both in the 1960s and the 1980s, McNamara and other NATO reformers believed that reducing reliance on nuclear elements of the force posture must be accompanied by a buildup in conventional forces. Indeed in November 1984, NATO adopted a new follow-on-forces-attack (FOFA) concept, which aims to make NATO conventional forces more effective in attacking rear echelon Warsaw Pact forces in the event of a Soviet attack on Western Europe.[13] The move is controversial, however, since it appears to transform what were manifestly defensive NATO forces into a more offensive posture, thereby threatening in peacetime one of the most basic Soviet security requirements: control over their East European buffer zone.[14]

Both NATO reformers and their critics alike may seriously

misjudge the requirements of extended deterrence, by overestimating the level of military force, and by underestimating the degree of political cohesion necessary to deter Soviet adventurism in Western Europe. NATO planners appear to base alliance force requirements, which determine and constrain NATO arms control possibilities, on several misplaced assumptions: (1) that the Soviets have an uncontrollable desire to expand territorially westward, and would have invaded Western Europe long ago in the absence of the U.S. commitment to retaliate to a Warsaw Pact conventional attack with nuclear weapons; (2) that the credibility of this retaliatory threat requires nuclear forces at least in balance with, and preferably superior to, the nuclear forces of the potential aggressor; and (3) that the American people will continue to support the effort to maintain nuclear superiority over the Soviet Union and the threat to initiate the first use of nuclear weapons since Hiroshima and Nagasaki.

These assumptions drive force requirements and, if correct, actually preclude effective arms control. Under these conditions the negotiation process will continue to be more competitive than cooperative, the allies will continue to suffer cycles of anxiety about the American nuclear umbrella, and the special interests opposed to arms restraint will continue to hamper U.S. arms control efforts. In the late 1980s, however, all three assumptions need to be reexamined.

Reassessing Assumption 1: Is There a Soviet Threat to Western Europe?

In the early 1950s, fear that the Korean War presaged a Soviet move into Western Europe was the primary stimulus behind the conventional rearmament of the NATO countries.[15] Since then, however, apart from some pressure on West Berlin in the late 1950s and early 1960s, there is little evidence that the Soviets have had either the opportunity or the urge to expand their sphere of influence westward.[16] On the contrary, since 1945 the Soviet leadership had been preoccupied with the effort to consolidate Eastern Europe as both a security and an ideological buffer against military threats and destabilizing influences from the West.

Maintaining control over Eastern Europe has been the sine qua non of Soviet security policy, but has proved to be an ex-

tremely demanding requirement. The Soviets have had to deploy their most highly trained forces and most up-to-date
equipment in the Warsaw Pact states, not only to deter an attack
from the NATO countries, but to impress East European Communist Party leaders and populations with the firmness of Soviet control over this vital buffer zone. The Soviets have also
provided many East European military units with modern
equipment, but this does not translate automatically into loyalty
to Moscow. The Warsaw Treaty Organization may appear to
have an impressive blitzkrieg capability on paper, but Soviet
leaders can hardly count on the Warsaw Pact armies for anything but defending East European territory—certainly not for
an offensive move into Western Europe.[17]

These occupation costs, together with the economic subsidies
to maintain the minimum living standards necessary to establish a modicum of legitimacy for the ruling Communist parties,
make Eastern Europe as much of an economic and military li-
ability for Moscow as it is a political asset. This suggests that the
next generation of Soviet leaders will be at least as likely as the
postwar generation have been to limit their role in Europe to
preventing any interference with either their military or political control over the Warsaw Pact states.[18]

Deterrence does not exist in a vacuum.[19] States run risks in
particular contexts for particular objectives and will always be
prepared to pay a higher price to defend positions and interests
than to expand them. Thus, while paranoid at their periphery,
the Soviets are merely opportunistic beyond it. Keeping the Soviets out of Western Europe therefore may well be a much less
demanding task than NATO planners now assume, because the
temptation for Soviet mischief is so low. Here, as elsewhere,
deterrence is much easier than compellence since the would-be
aggressor must initiate the process of changing the status quo
and suffer the initial burden of risk. Recall that in the late
1940s, the Western powers were deterred from pushing the Soviets out of Eastern Europe—despite an American nuclear monopoly—by the prospect of engaging Stalin's war-torn armies
in conventional battle.[20] For a nation as risk-averse as the Soviets have proved to be, any move into Western Europe would
have to be a last-ditch effort to avert the imminent collapse of
Soviet control over Eastern Europe, or an imminent attack
from the West. Even under those dire circumstances, Soviet
planners contemplating military action would have to weigh not

only NATO's capability to resist attack, but also the United States' resolve to defend its sustained interest and substantial investment in the territorial and political integrity of Western Europe.

As Michael Howard wrote, criticizing those who argued that the new Soviet SS-20 missiles undermined the credibility of the American security guarantee (emphasis added),

There is no consensus in the European defense community, and there is no sense among the European people as a whole that the SS-20s present a threat of a new order of magnitude. *The United States is "coupled" to Europe not by one delivery system or another, but by a vast web of military installations and personnel, to say nothing of the innumerable economic social and financial links that tie us together into a single coherent system.*[21]

NATO nevertheless proceeded to shore up an imagined nuclear deficiency in its military force posture, thereby generating an outpouring of antinuclear and anti-American sentiment in Western Europe that seriously compromised the "single coherent system" and the political cohesion on which—as Howard rightly claims—extended deterrence rests.

Rather than focusing exclusively on military capabilities, both the Soviets' to attack and NATO's to resist, NATO leaders should be more sensitive to the dangers of an alliance in political disarray being perceived by a potential aggressor as a tempting target. Today, as in the prenuclear era, the degree to which great powers see any advantage in initiating military activity against each other's allies rests largely on the perception each has of the other's capability and resolve to defend its protegés, be they formally or only loosely allied.[22] When an alliance appears cohesive there is less temptation to attack its member states militarily or probe alliance differences politically. If the interests of alliance members begin to diverge, however, an adversary is tempted to exploit the rift by intervening in intra-alliance debates on sensitive issues, setting off one ally against another and generally undermining alliance cohesion. This tendency is manifest in both Soviet behavior toward NATO and U.S. behavior toward the Warsaw Pact.

Thus, in the early 1980s, even as he denounced strikes by air traffic controllers at home, President Reagan enthusiastically supported strikes by the independent Polish trade union Solidarity. Industrial unrest in Poland not only challenged Communist Party rule in that country, but also tended to undermine Soviet control over Poland in particular and over Eastern Europe generally. Similarly, as West Europeans took to the streets to protest their governments' willingness to provide bases for the new American cruise and Pershing II missiles (mandated by NATO's "double-track" decision of December 1979), the Soviets stepped up their carrot-and-stick campaign against NATO by threatening dire retribution against those states that accepted the new missiles, and less drastic treatment for nuclear-free states. With East German Communist Party leader Erich Honecker assigned a key role, the Soviets also mounted a carefully orchestrated campaign against the INF deployments in West Germany, intervening with clumsy and ultimately counterproductive tactics in the March 1983 federal elections.

In the extreme case, alliance interests could diverge so far that one superpower would appear to have abandoned its commitment to defend its allies' interests. An adversary might then be tempted to go beyond political mischief and initiate military actions against a weak and abandoned protegé, confident that the guarantor state—despite its capability to do so—would not retaliate. An alliance in disarray could thus tempt a would-be aggressor to act militarily in a crisis.

Thus, while the threat of nuclear retaliation would not be an insignificant factor in deterring Soviet adventurism in a crisis, NATO's cohesion, in terms of effectively integrated forces in Western Europe and manifest commonality of political and economic interests between the United States and Western Europe, is the crucial component of the western deterrent. NATO policy should therefore concentrate both on increasing political cohesion in the alliance and on removing any temptation for Soviet military action in a crisis. This objective should inform both alliance force planning and alliance diplomacy at the two multilateral negotiations on European security: the interalliance talks in Vienna on Mutual and Balanced Force Reductions, and the pan-European Conference on Security and Confidence-Building Measures in Stockholm.

For the United States this means, above all, conducting a foreign policy that makes American interest in defending the integrity of Western Europe unambiguous, so as not to tempt the Soviets. This means as far as possible eliminating transatlantic squabbles about trade and monetary policy, defense burden sharing, and technology transfers to the East bloc. It also means abstaining from patterns of deployment in Western Europe that suggest an offensive-looking NATO posture that might threaten Soviet control over Eastern Europe. Few if any NATO governments want anything but the most gradual evolution in Eastern Europe, and to suggest by deep strike force postures or inflammatory rhetoric either the capability or the intention to change the political or territorial status quo in Eastern Europe by force is not only provocative to the Soviets but profoundly unsettling to the allies. A revival of interest in creating a stronger European pillar in NATO reflected the unhappiness with American leadership of the alliance across a broad political spectrum in Western Europe in the mid-1980s.

Reassessing Assumption 2: The Need for Balanced Nuclear Forces

U.S. policy has rested on the assumption that the credibility of the American security guarantee to NATO—specifically the threat to retaliate with nuclear weapons to a conventional Warsaw Pact attack—requires nuclear forces at least in balance with and preferably superior to those of the Soviet Union. Indeed this is the primary motor that drives the acquisition and modernization of the U.S. nuclear arsenal.[23] It is an assumption strengthened by the traditional arms control process, which seeks balanced agreements with reciprocal rights and obligations. It is mirrored by the Soviet preoccupation with maintaining parity with the United States to demonstrate a positive correlation of forces in favor of the socialist camp. Moreover, most of the public interest groups that lobby for arms control, including those supporting the nuclear freeze, subscribe to the concept of balance. Brave indeed is the elected official who dares to suggest even the most modest measures of unilateral restraint. Even the American Catholic bishops' pastoral letter, which argues at length the immorality of any purpose for nuclear weapons except deterrence, nevertheless asserts the need for "deterrence based on balance."

Balance only makes sense, however, in militarily useful systems. Yet, four decades into the nuclear era, despite the best efforts of civilian strategists and game theorists, the military have not been able to devise any rational missions for nuclear explosives. Neither military nor political purposes can be served by escalating from nonnuclear to nuclear use.[24] The devastation from blast, heat, and radiation is too immense, and the costs of a nuclear war unimaginable. Thus, regardless of relative capability, we have a state of what McGeorge Bundy has called "existential deterrence." In addition to the effects long anticipated in the northern hemisphere from an East-West nuclear war, studies by atmospheric scientists now suggest the possibility of catastrophic global effects on climate from massive emissions of smoke and toxic chemicals following a major nuclear exchange. The global population is thus now at the mercy of the nuclear weapons powers. These risks will not go away, nor will they be materially changed by advances in technology, fluctuations in relative nuclear capability, or changes in military doctrine on either side. This is the essence of the nuclear revolution.[25]

If nuclear explosives have no military utility, and their only practical purpose is for deterrence, this can be achieved by a force of a few hundred warheads at most, each of which can credibly threaten to destroy a city.[26] To be deterred from provoking what would be a devasting retaliatory strike, the would-be aggressor only needs to know this deterrent force is invulnerable. Some analysts claim that while such a force might be sufficient to deter a direct nuclear attack on the United States, it would not necessarily serve to deter a Warsaw Pact conventional attack on Western Europe.[27] But, as Dennis Healey observed in the 1960s, credibility is not symmetrical between potential attackers and defenders. A 95% likelihood that the United States would respond to a conventional Warsaw Pact attack with nuclear weapons might not be enough to reassure the West Europeans of the American commitment, but only a 5% chance of such a response could be more than enough to deter the Russians.[28] As already noted, one state extends its deterrent capabilities over another not by increasing its military capability but by demonstrating a closer political affinity with its protegé.[29]

Yet far from coming to terms with our permanent vulnerability, NATO strategists vainly try to refine alliance doctrine by searching for implementable threats. In particular, strategists have tried to move away from the apparently immoral threat to target the adversary's civilian populations in cities, to the seemingly more benign strategy of targeting the enemy's military forces. But the distinction between countercity and counterforce targeting is not operationally feasible. Despite recent attempts to produce smaller, "cleaner" nuclear explosives, any effective nuclear counterforce strike would also kill unacceptably large sections of the population and could hardly be viewed as "limited" by the state under attack.

The fact that nuclear weapons are simply too powerful to be used must be faced and the logical conclusions drawn, namely:

• nuclear explosives are not military weapons—they are simply nuclear explosives;

• nuclear superiority is not military superiority—it is simply nuclear superiority;

• deterrence of aggression by other nuclear powers requires only a few hundred nuclear explosives based in invulnerable delivery vehicles;

• beyond this absolute capability, relative nuclear strength is irrelevant to our security and the security of our allies;

• the search for nuclear balance is meaningless;

• there is nothing irresponsible, or dangerous, about reducing our nuclear arsenals unilaterally;

• nuclear explosives cannot substitute for conventional forces and in no way compensate for conventional inadequacy;

• therefore, reducing current nuclear arsenals does not imply a reduction in military capability and does not require any compensatory increase in conventional strength;

• on the contrary, removing nuclear weapons commingled with NATO ground forces will actually increase the conventional capability of those units by releasing manpower currently preoccupied with the custody of nuclear warheads.

Reassessing Assumption 3: Continued Public Support for NATO's Nuclear Policy

Since its inception, NATO doctrine and force planning has been in the hands of a relatively small community of defense experts. Politically, the strongest transatlantic bonds are between British, West German, and American officials and analysts of the center-right, with an especially conservative coterie dominating policy in the late 1970s.[30] This group formulated NATO's double-track decision to modernize and control intermediate-range nuclear forces (INF), which, as already noted, focused on shoring up misperceived inadequacies in the nuclear component of NATO's deterrent at the expense of alliance cohesion.

The early 1980s were thus marked by growing anxiety on both sides of the Atlantic about the dangers of nuclear war and a profound rethinking of the tenets of alliance doctrine across the political spectrum. Of particular concern toward the end of the Carter presidency was the emphasis on limited nuclear options, and the stated requirements for a capability to fight and prevail in a nuclear war so as to be able to dominate every rung on a hypothetical ladder of escalation.[31] Later, the public, and much of the expert community as well, grew increasingly disturbed by the primitive anti-Soviet rhetoric, and loose talk of nuclear use, among senior appointees in the Reagan administration. The public outcry to the decision to deploy 572 new INF warheads on cruise and Pershing II missiles in Western Europe, capable of striking Soviet targets, demonstrated the wide disparity between the experts' and the public view of what couples the United States to Western Europe. The experts claimed the new missiles would ease NATO's fears of abandonment by coupling U.S. and West European security more closely together. By contrast, most Europeans believed that cruise and Pershing IIs increase the risk of nuclear war by presenting attractive targets to Soviet forces: a classic fear of entrapment anxiety to which the experts seemed quite insensitive. These European anxieties were not eased when the Reagan administration eventually began to implement the negotiation track of the double-track decision. On the contrary, the manifest lack of interest in Washington in concluding an equitable INF agreement made it clear that the earlier promise of negotiations had been primarily a fig leaf for deployments.

A number of retired officials, from government and military service in the NATO countries, are among the new nuclear skeptics.[32] They complain of many aspects of NATO policy, including the fact that nuclear war fighting plans are dangerously unrealistic, that targeting policy and military training tend to dehumanize the adversary, that inside assessments of the Soviet threat do not sufficiently take into account Soviet security requirements, and that NATO's nuclear emphasis is often at the expense of prudent conventional force planning.

In Western Europe, antinuclear activists from the late 1950s and early 1960s joined forces with newly aroused professional and grass-roots organizations, including very active church-based groups. In the United States, architects, educators, environmentalists, lawyers, musicians, scientists, and physicians formed antinuclear groups, all of which supported the national campaign to freeze the testing, production, and deployment of Soviet and American nuclear arsenals. The Protestant Church had long been critical of American nuclear policy, but now the U.S. Catholic Conference also became involved.

In May 1983, a Pastoral Letter on War and Peace sought to place defense policy in the context of Catholic teaching on the requirements for a just war.[33] In particular, the bishops emphasized the need to discriminate between combatants and noncombatants, and the need for proportionality between military means and political ends. The gist of the pastoral letter was to delegitimize any use of nuclear weapons—whether first or second, early or late—since the bishops concluded that even if ostensibly aimed at military targets, nuclear explosives would destroy millions of noncombatants, and no one could be certain that, once begun, a nuclear exchange could be kept limited. The bishops were unambiguous in their support for a bilateral nuclear freeze and for a NATO no-first-use policy, and echoed the judgment of Pope John Paul II at the second United Nations Special Session on Disarmament in June 1982 that possession of nuclear weapons for the purpose of deterring others was morally acceptable only as an interim measure on the way to disarmament.

The freeze movement, the new professional activists, and the bishops' letter in the United States, as well as the various facets of the antinuclear movement in Western Europe, raised public consciousness on the nuclear issue on both sides of the Atlantic. Public opinion surveys revealed substantial majorities opposing NATO's nuclear policies in the early 1980s. Most of those polled in NATO Europe, for example, opposed the deployment of new cruise and Pershing II INF missiles.[34] In the United States surveys showed a massive shift in sentiment from the 1950s, when most Americans believed nuclear weapons served the cause of peace, to the current fears that Soviet and American nuclear arsenals are increasing the risk of war and eroding international security.[35]

In the late 1940s and early 1950s, most Americans approved of the bombing of Hiroshima and Nagasaki and believed the United States could fight, win, and survive a nuclear war. In

1984, by contrast, most Americans thought a nuclear war would be uncontrollable and suicidal.

In the mid-1950s, most Americans felt it was justified to retaliate with nuclear weapons to a nonnuclear Soviet attack on Western Europe. In 1984, by contrast, 77% of those polled said the United States should not initiate the use of nuclear weapons in response to a conventional attack on the allies, and 74% believed nuclear weapons should never be used in a battlefield situation. Most Americans seemed unaware that current NATO policy threatens the first use of nuclear weapons. In one survey 81 percent of those polled believed that it is U.S. policy to use nuclear weapons if and only if the Soviets use them first.

In the 1950s, most Americans felt that nuclear superiority enhanced national security. In 1984, they understood that the Russians had caught up, and would build to keep up, so that regaining American superiority was no longer a feasible option. More than 75% accepted this nuclear stalemate and supported a bilateral nuclear freeze as the best route to getting nuclear weapons under control, while 61% saw no risk in a unilateral moratorium on new American systems, hoping the Soviets would follow suit.

Finally, in contrast to earlier surveys, most Americans now believed that acquiring extra nuclear weapons as bargaining chips for negotiations was counterproductive, serving only to generate Soviet countermeasures.

The impact of all this antinuclear sentiment is hard to gauge. In the United States, the House of Representatives voted against the MX missile in 1982 and endorsed the nuclear freeze in 1983, as did the Democratic Party for its 1984 election platform. But only a few legislators supported efforts to legislate a delay in INF deployments in 1983. NATO leaders claim to be reducing reliance on nuclear weapons, but talk of modernizing battlefield weapons even as obsolete ones are being withdrawn. Furthermore, the restructuring of conventional forces to conform with the follow-on-forces-attack concept could generate as many problems in East-West relations as it was supposed to solve within the alliance.[36]

Election results in the United States suggest that most nuclear freeze proponents vote their pocketbooks and their ambivalence about the Soviet Union, rather than their anxieties about nuclear war. In Britain and West Germany in the early 1980s federal elections were all won by conservatives committed to free enterprise, a tougher stand on the Russians, and no delays in the INF deployments. It should be noted, however, that the main opposition parties in all these elections were those that, when in office in the late 1970s, had previously either called for—or approved—new land-based nuclear missiles in Europe that could strike Soviet targets—the Democratic, Labour, and Social Democratic Parties, respectively. So it could be said that voters in these three countries were hardly offered convincing alternatives or attractive choices on the nuclear issue.

If the antinuclear impact on the ballot box was mixed, the INF decision and subsequent protest nevertheless had a disturbing effect on alliance cohesion. Polling data suggest that antinuclear sentiment is far from synonomous with anti-NATO sentiment. Nevertheless, much of the opposition to INF was bitterly anti-American and did raise transatlantic hackles as the European left and the American isolationist right reinforced the stereotypes each had of the other. In the United States, this generated a new crop of congressional resolutions calling for the withdrawal of American troops from Europe and complaints that the Europeans were not pulling their weight in NATO burden sharing, while in Western Europe, the INF debacle—in both its Carter and its Reagan phases—contributed to the decline in respect for American leadership in handling world affairs and a growing skepticism and weakened attachment to NATO among the more highly educated.[37]

NATO governments, by and large, continued to support and implement the INF decision despite growing opposition in those states designated to receive the new missiles, but they often did so with embarrassingly close margins in their legislatures.

In West Germany, Chancellor Helmut Schmidt first raised the alarm about a Eurostrategic imbalance in the mid-1970s, and supported the INF decision while in office. In opposition, however, Schmidt's Social Democratic Party denounced INF deployments in 1983 and endorsed a no-first-use policy for NATO in May 1984. Greece dissociated itself from the INF decision, the Netherlands voted to delay deployment of its allotted share of cruise missiles, and Denmark voted against paying its share of the INF infrastructure costs.

In Britain, Mrs. Thatcher's government held firm, but the Labour Party opposition—despite the Callaghan government having approved cruise in the late 1970s—condemned the INF decision in the early 1980s and vowed to remove cruise and Pershing if and when the Labour Party returned to office. The British Liberal Party broke ranks with its Social Democratic Party partner to condemn INF, voted against continuation of an independent British deterrent, and endorsed a no-first-use policy for NATO.

Conclusion

Several policy recommendations emerge from this analysis of the alliance arms control dilemma and the requirements for extended deterrence:

European anxieties about the U.S. commitment to NATO are best assuaged by political rather than by military measures. This is because the collective security of the NATO countries, not only in terms of reassuring the West Europeans but also in deterring military moves by the Warsaw Pact, rests at least as much on political cohesion as on strictly military capabilities.

As long as NATO relies heavily on the nuclear component of its force posture, bilateral Soviet-U.S. efforts to control nuclear systems will continue to trigger fears of abandonment in some Europeans and attempts to ease these fears with nuclear hardware will inevitably trigger fear of entrapment, a new bout of anti-Americanism, and intraalliance tensions. European calls for reassurance should therefore be dealt with politically. In the arms control context this will mean either improving intra-alliance consultations or bringing the allies directly into the negotiations so that they share responsibility for the outcome. The long-term solution, however, is to recognize that nuclear weapons have always been divisive in alliance politics, that nuclear explosives cannot defend territory and certainly cannot defend heavily urban Western Europe, and that far from enhancing NATO's deterrent capability, land-based nuclear systems on the continent are more likely to provoke Soviet preemption in a crisis.

Second, NATO doctrine should recognize that nuclear weapons can only serve a deterrent function, for which balanced nuclear forces are not required. NATO should decide on the absolute level of its deterrent force and withdraw redundant systems in as orderly a manner as possible, preferably in cooperation with the Soviet Union, but recognizing that unilateral reductions need not undermine either U.S. or West European security. As outlined earlier, nuclear explosives are not military weapons and should not be treated as such either by making plans for their use in battle or by insisting that nuclear arms control agreements be balanced.

Third, in reducing reliance on the nuclear component of the deterrent, NATO planners should not make the nonnuclear component more offensive. This is the risk inherent in proposals for a NATO declaration on the no-first-use of nuclear weapons, since it is usually coupled with a call for stronger conventional forces. Proponents claim that the threat of first-use has lost its former credibility since Soviet-American parity makes any nuclear use suicidal. For West European leaders still leaning on the nuclear crutch, however, a no-first-use declaration triggers fears of abandonment in the event of a Soviet attack. Ideally, then, the shift to no-first-use should be preceded by an MBFR agreement setting limits on Soviet manpower in Eastern Europe. Pulling back both sides' battlefield theater nuclear forces and armored divisions would further reduce the offensive threat to both halves of Europe and make no-first-use still more acceptable. This kind of restructuring might be difficult to achieve by contractual limits because the compliance obligations would be asymmetrical. Nevertheless it is the kind of mutual offsetting of asymmetries that ought to be discussed, both at MBRF in Vienna and at the CSCBM conference in Stockholm.

Fourth, reductions of American troops or nuclear weapons from Western Europe are better negotiated with the Western allies than with the Soviet Union. Negotiations aimed at arms control agreements with adversaries generate fears of abandonment in the allies and rarely achieve more than a codification of the status quo. Major reductions of military forces are usually unilateral measures after political settlements, or changes in military doctrine when the forces in question have become redundant. The withdrawal of 2,400 American nuclear warheads formerly assigned to battlefield weapons in western Europe, negotiated within NATO, thus provides a better arms control model than the bilateral Soviet-American talks on nuclear weapons.

Finally, political leaders should be aware that public opinion on both sides of the Atlantic is ready for bolder steps to reduce the danger of nuclear war. Furthermore, the most impressive arms control achievements to date—the Limited Test Ban Treaty, the ABM Treaty, and the Biological Weapons Convention—came not from initiatives from the so-called "experts," but primarily from strong grass-roots pressure and from political leaders willing to take bold unilateral initiatives. The current generation of Western leaders should not hesitate to dismantle redundant systems and to negotiate freeze agreements with the Soviet Union designed to preclude deployment of the next generation of nuclear weapons.

5

Nuclear Crisis and Human Frailty
Lincoln P. Bloomfield

The Fourth "C" in C³: Crisis

A foreign policy crisis has three characteristics: important values are threatened; decisions are urgent; and it usually takes policymakers by surprise.

All crises are not necessarily bad. Given the tendency of foreign affairs bureaucracies to procrastinate and to shun long-term planning (Bloomfield's Law says "nothing happens in Washington until it has to"), a crisis can sometimes be beneficial. Harlan Cleveland observed two decades ago while U.S. ambassador to NATO that basic foreign policy decisions are often made in crises.[1] Former Secretary of State Henry A. Kissinger celebrated the virtues of crisis decision making as clarifying the diplomatic landscape while suppressing irritating secondary details.[2] Lenin, in an undoubtedly inadvertent coincidence, asserted that "all crises bring out the essence of phenomena . . . sweeping aside the superficial, petty, and external."[3] And the late strategist Herman Kahn thought that limited world government would probably come about via a telephone call between U.S. and Soviet leaders following a nuclear exchange.

Crises that arise in the nuclear age inescapably carry with them the possibility, however remote, that someone will think about using nuclear weapons. Students of post-World War II crises debate whether Washington or Moscow ever seriously contemplated such a portentous step. President Eisenhower reportedly threatened their possible use in the Korean War. But the weight of the evidence so far has supported the conclusion drawn by the presidential National Security Adviser during the hairiest decade (so far) of nuclear crisis diplomacy. Reflecting on his White House service, McGeorge Bundy wrote,

There is an enormous gulf between what political leaders really think about nuclear weapons and what is assumed in . . . simulated strategic warfare. In the real world of real political leaders—whether here or in the Soviet Union—a decision that would bring one hydrogen bomb on one city of one's country would be recognized in advance as a catastrophic blunder; ten bombs on ten cities would be a disaster beyond history. . . .[4]

Crises are not abstractions. One kind of scenario—the nightmare of a deliberately planned "bolt from the blue" surprise attack—has become massively deterred (although not inconceivable). The nature of the Soviet system fosters probes and tests of nerve, but few expect the Soviet assault on Western Europe for which the West has long prepared. The most probable scenario is an escalating "local conflict" in a turbulent region of the world where the United States and U.S.S.R. take opposite sides—the endless Arab-Israeli war (which has already featured several superpower crises), the Persian Gulf, southern Africa, and perhaps East Asia or the Caribbean. There will be civil violence by groups one side calls "terrorist" and the other "freedom fighters." And we cannot rule out such hitherto unlikely Eurasian scenarios as German reunification efforts, Sino-Soviet hostilities, and turmoil in Eastern Europe or Soviet Central Asia.

Whatever arms control or normalization of relations may be achieved, the only prudent bet is for a future punctuated by crises that both the White House and the Kremlin must somehow manage without at some point losing their cool and reaching for genocidal weapons. For this reason nuclear crisis management belongs close to the top of the "peace and security" agenda. So long as there are nuclear weapons—and crises—the paramount goal of national security policy must be *stability in crisis situations,* a point stressed by the Scowcroft Commission when it argued that "the first (arms control) goal should be to ensure that the nature of the forces on each side does not provide a military incentive to strike first with nuclear weapons in a crisis."[5] The conclusion of six U.S. participants in the Cuban Missile Crisis was that "in any crisis involving the superpowers, firm control by the heads of both governments is essential to the avoidance of an unpredictably escalating conflict."[6]

So far the nuclear superpowers have been able to ride out crises, however serious, without great pressure to use nuclear weapons. *There was always time to find out what was really happening and to conduct diplomacy aimed at cooling things down.* The management of crisis will, however, soon acquire some deeply unsettling characteristics. At worst, they raise urgent questions about the capacity of the political leadership in Washington and Moscow to handle future crises with the nuclear restraint they have shown thus far.

Pinpoint accuracies and close-in missile deployments have already produced fears of being caught out. If a crisis arose in an already tense period, decision makers would have made preparations to retain control. But they would be under almost unprecedented pressure, and in the next few years it might begin to seem less insane than before to launch one's most vulnerable missiles before the other side could land explosives on them. It is not that a nuclear attack would have any greater certainty of "success" than before. And accidental nuclear detonations would be virtually ruled out by technical precautions. But under circumstances it is not hard to envisage, uncertainty may no longer be on the side of deterrence.

National leaders understandably profess confidence in their ability to control crises. But recent U.S. presidents including Ronald Reagan have proposed to Moscow measures aimed at reducing the danger of war by miscalculation. The Soviets for their part are usually inhibited from admitting the non-Marxist possibility of losing control. But more recently they agreed to discuss "crisis-reduction centers," and Central Committee member Georgi Arbatov wrote that "in a world where international tension is the rule . . . states may be drawn quite unintentionally into a sequence of events in which eventually they lose control over the situation and it becomes impossible to prevent a catastrophe."[7]

For the United States, good control requires that in tense circumstances the president be able reliably to communicate with nuclear forces worldwide, while receiving timely intelligence. To achieve that involves a vast collection of people, sensors, command centers, electronics, and information summed up in the jargon as "C^3I," pronounced see-cubed-eye, and spelled out as Command, Control, Communications, and Intelligence. Our concern here is with the first three.

Three developments have combined to focus urgent attention on C^3. One is the phenomenal improvement in the accuracy of the thousands of nuclear warheads deployed worldwide. Second, such weapons are targeted on each side's retaliatory forces, and deployed ever closer to both sides' command centers. The effect of that is steadily to shrink warning time of potential attack from days to hours to minutes. Third, the information flow essential to rational decisions has vastly multiplied throughout the network that includes telephone lines, switching centers, radar antennae, and presidents of the United States. But at the same time that network is increasingly vulnerable to accurately aimed nuclear blast, electromagnetic pulses, "decapitation" aimed at national leadership, and the chaos likely to follow explosion in anger of a nuclear weapon for the first time since 1945.

Enormous technical efforts are underway to offset such threats to the ability to manage future nuclear crises. C^3 in total consumed \$25 billion of a recent U.S. defense budget. Those efforts are eminently justifiable. But perhaps the most worrisome component of crisis management—the *human* factor—is the least analyzed or even acknowledged. Yet unless nuclear crisis management is to be turned over to computers, fateful decisions are going to be made under conditions of unprecedented stress by fallible, failure-prone human beings.

The dual problem of crisis stability can be symbolized by a simple equation. On one side of the equal sign is the military hardware, the C^3 technology, and the time available to make discriminatory judgments. On the other side is a human head, with what one hopes is a normal brain between the ears.

Such an equation for crisis management in 1955 would have shown on the "hardware" side a stockpile of crude atomic bombs deliverable by subsonic bombers; commercial telephone and cable companies conveying a torrent of messages flowing in and out of headquarters; and a nerve-racking "worst case" requirement to make fateful decisions within hours. On the other side of the equation was the human decision maker.

Now picture a similar equation for, say, 1990. On the left side is an exponentially increased number of nuclear warheads aboard thousands of large and small missiles, ships, planes, and gun carriages. Information about events (and nonevents) comes in a tidal wave of instantaneously processed data. The "worst case" requirement for fateful decisions is now not hours, but minutes—perhaps no more than five. But on the right side of the 1990 equation is the same old unimproved model of the human head.

The analysis that follows asks what kind of "critical mass" might form when the two sides of the equation—state-of-the-art space age technology, and old-fashioned human beings—are brought together in a future nuclear crisis. After examining the facts and proposed remedies, one is left with a nagging feeling that the laudable effort to upgrade C³, if not accompanied by major policy changes, may have the perverse effect of hastening our slide toward a world, foreseen by psychiatrist Eric Fromm, of "impotent men directed by virile machines."

The Trend toward "Crisis Instability"

Nuclear deterrent strategy, whatever its long-term shortcomings, has so far worked, even under grave provocation. It is rooted in the ability to inflict intolerable damage regardless of what someone else may do first. No less crucial to successful deterrence is the *belief* that this is true. Both capability and belief have so far kept the "strategic panic" threshold sufficiently high for superpower leadership, when faced with an intense crisis, to stay relatively cool while waiting to see what happens and how to get out of it gracefully.

In crises ranging from Korea, Suez, and Hungary in the 1950s and Berlin and Cuba in the 1960s, to the Middle East, Afghanistan, and Poland in the 1970s and 1980s, Soviet and American crisis managers were able to make their military and diplomatic moves without crippling worries about being rendered militarily impotent by a preemptive nuclear strike. Even more to the point, when decision makers were faced with ambiguous information implying a *possible* attack—worrisome troop movements, suggestive radar echoes, satellite failures, whatever—the policymakers could still wait for confirmation without being stampeded or panicked into an unintentional and unwanted war.

It is not always appreciated how burdensome is the *information load* in a major foreign policy crisis, and how demanding on the human mind. Top-level attention is suddenly focused on diplomatic cable traffic and military intelligence that would normally stop at lower levels. Leaders trying to think clearly suddenly confront complex choices while being constantly interrupted with urgent messages. As high-speed electronic processing of information automates the flow, the burden on the top layer of the decision pyramid, already a chronic victim of information overload, becomes overwhelming.

In addition, at the very time when subtlety comes hardest, decision makers also must scan the flow of events for *symbolic* moves by the other side. A shift of certain military units may signal offensive intentions—or be a tacit reassurance that nothing is planned. Words left out of a diplomatic message or use of private channels may—or may not—communicate an intention to change course. The Kremlin sometimes prefers indirect or "deniable" communication in a crisis, as in its astonishing use of a private American journalist (John Scali) at the height of the Cuban Missile Crisis, or the signals when Moscow was ready to wind down the Korean War but did not want to say so publicly (Secretary of State Acheson called that message "sibylline"[8]). Such signals are extraordinarily hard to decipher, culturally opaque, and subject to serious misinterpretation or even being totally missed.

At such times a generous amount of *mis*information is also available to the decision maker. Intelligence agents around the world want to earn their keep, and a torrent of unconfirmed but worrisome reports piles in faster than it can be absorbed, let alone checked out. Two egregious examples were the "sightings" of Soviet submarines and overflying aircraft during the dual crises of Suez and Hungary in 1956, and the ambiguous buildup of Soviet forces in the Trans-Caucasus Military District after the invasion of Afghanistan in late 1979, raising the fateful possibility that Iran would be next. In these and other cases the "prudent assessment" turned out to be incorrect. In a full-blown nuclear crisis, even normal precautionary responses to ambiguous information could be catastrophically wrong.

Accidental firings of nuclear weapons are most unlikely. But other kinds of "accidents" have triggered military alerts on both sides. They range from the rising of the moon and flights of geese misinterpreted by the newly installed BMEWS early warning radars in the far north, through accidental running of practice nuclear alarm tapes at NORAD—the U.S.-Canadian North American Aerospace Defense Command in Cheyenne Mountain, Colorado—to a 1984 presidential quip into a presumably dead microphone about bombing the Soviet Union.

Literature and drama went further and imagined an Armageddon based on the vulnerability of the system to a deranged unit commander, defective microchip, misunderstood piece of intelligence, or communications garble between American and Soviet leaders. These have so far been fiction, and the reassuring reality was that U.S. and Soviet leadership could safely wait out any crisis while double-checking information, calling for confirmation, conducting diplomacy, even gambling on high-risk moves (as with Khrushchev and Kennedy in the Cuban Missile Crisis, and Brezhnev and Nixon/Kissinger during the Yom Kippur War in November 1973). During the first three post-World War II decades, both superpowers acquired large and diverse nuclear arsenals. But there were still no real "first-strike" weapons, despite loose use of that phrase. There still are none in the sense of depriving the victim of a credible capacity to retaliate with intolerable damage. There was and still is "crisis stability."

Those days may soon be over.

The Shrinkage in Decision-Making Time

If the national crisis decision-making system is to work in a worst case, the following things must happen. Multiple, possibly ambiguous warnings of an impending attack must be processed and evaluated. In the United States the president must be found and informed. He has to decide whether to believe or disbelieve the available evidence, and, if the evidence is unequivocal, authorize a response. That presidential authorization must be transmitted to worldwide launch control centers. Missile and bomber crews underground, in the air, aboard ship, underwater, or in the field must believe that this time they really have to turn the keys necessary to arm and fire nuclear weapons.

The most profound threat to rational decision making will come from the steady shrinkage of time in which to do all this—learn, evaluate, and respond—under crisis conditions.

The drift toward crisis instability began with the development of MIRV—multiple independently targetable warheads—which could theoretically knock out not just one but many targets from which retaliation might come. In the same period missile guidance systems became extraordinarily accurate. Cities had always been at risk. But now, with delivery systems precise enough to dig a missile or command post out of its hardened shelter and versatile enough to cover a large fraction of the opponent's nuclear forces, the decisive targets would be strategic nuclear arsenals, and the strategy one of "counter-force" rather than city-busting.

If each superpower's land-based ICBMs cut the other's deci-sion-making time from many hours to 30 minutes, intermedi-ate-range missiles, such as the U.S. Pershing IIs in Europe and those carried by offshore Soviet Yankee-class submarines, can reach critical headquarters targets in a handful of minutes. It is not that 30 minutes is much more time than 10, or that some retaliatory systems would not remain intact. It is that new ac-curacies, plus targeting and launching doctrines, may force hu-man choices in even less time than before.

There are other candidates for crisis destabilization. Both sides depend on early warning and communications satellites not just for military purposes but for reassurance that there is no need to go to war. But if antisatellite weapons are not out-lawed, they will soon be vulnerable, contributing to instability in crisis. Further into the future, effective antisubmarine war-fare could put the prime U.S. retaliatory force at risk.

The U.S. Strategic Defense Initiative—nicknamed "Star Wars"—envisaging a layered ballistic missile defense, is also po-tentially destabilizing. Certainly an effective two-sided missile defense would be morally preferable to massive offensive retal-iation. But the danger lies in the *process*. In an *uneven* defense race, one side could be panicked into a preemptive strike dur-ing a crisis by concern that the other no longer felt vulnerable and thus was no longer thoroughly deterred.

Finally, military doctrines can contribute to instability. Soviet military literature has long featured articles on how to win even a nuclear war, including a doctrine of preemptive attack com-plete with "launch on warning" (although with authority to do so withheld until given),[9] plus warnings that a nuclear war could not be limited.[10] For its part, U.S. strategy, starting with Defense Secretary McNamara's Ann Arbor speech in 1962 through pronouncements by Secretaries Schlesinger and Rumsfeld during the Ford administration and further direc-tives by both Presidents Carter and Reagan, has envisaged a kind of calibrated nuclear war-fighting featuring "limited nu-clear options." At the same time, both superpowers reportedly have considered strategies of "decapitation" of the other side's political-military command centers, putting into question the capacity to control catastrophic escalation. Such doctrines emphasizing capabilities are meant to deter. Yet when it comes to assessing the other side's *intentions,* the deep-seated American determination to avoid another Pearl Harbor seems to be as unpersuasive to Moscow as Russia's long experience with invasions is to Washington.

The conclusion seems inescapable that before long, unless present trends are altered, leaders worried about imminent extinction when faced with ambiguous information, obscure signals, and possible technical malfunctions may no longer feel able to wait for greater certainty before committing at least some of their nuclear forces. The current U.S. solution to this grim dilemma, apart from new weapons systems to offset present or potential threats, takes the form of heroic efforts to upgrade the technology of command, control, and communication—C³.

The Problem of Keeping Control

The experts approach the C³ problem in two quite different ways. For some, the goal is to "prevail," employing a game of nuclear chicken along the classic blackmail lines of "one of us has to be rational and it's not going to be me." If one's primary aim is nuclear "escalation dominance," C³ upgrading is to enable the United States to wage not only a limited but a protracted nuclear war, on the theory that even in a nation-crushing exchange, if you can control your own nuclear forces, you can come out "ahead."

Others who consider that approach a dangerous fantasy favor C³ upgrading to be in a position to negotiate with the other side to end an unplanned, unwanted, and potentially suicidal superpower military confrontation before it spins out of control.

The design of U.S. nuclear decision making has walked the line since the 1940s between a pair of competing pressures: on one hand, greater centralization so the president can retain tight control over any use of nuclear weapons; and on the other hand, *de*centralization so the system is not paralyzed by a communications snafu or a terrified (or incinerated) president.

The C³ system has in fact compromised between those two criteria. The authority to order use of nuclear weapons belongs to the president. Unlike the constitutional succession, nuclear "release authority" descends from the president to the Defense secretary and deputy and service secretaries, all constituting the "National Command Authorities" (NCA).[11]

The president is linked on the "input" side to major warning systems and on the"output" side to Strategic Air Command (SAC), Readiness Command, and Central Command, plus theater commands such as those in Europe and the Pacific. His orders go from the National Military Command Center (NMCC)—the nation's war-room in the Pentagon linking all commands, sensors, nuclear burst detectors, radars, and radio frequencies—via the secretary of defense through the chairman of the Joint Chiefs of Staff.[12] In addition, since President Kennedy's time the White House Situation Room has been equipped to receive all important traffic and can communicate directly to virtually all points.[13]

Since the atomic age began, substantial effort has been invested in creating checks and balances in the nuclear decision-making system. The SAC commander may order the deployment of his B-52 bomber force on receipt of a credible warning from NORAD, but "positive launch control" keeps planes in airborne holding positions until Emergency Action Messages (EAMs) containing "Go" codes are received. Presumably the same is true of the submarine fleet, although communications difficulties in crisis make it possible for a submarine on its own to launch.[14] One of the crucial elements in the positive command and control system, although only for the U.S. land and air-based forces, is the array of computer-constructed electronic key codes, coding devices and interlocks—so-called "Permissive Action Links" (PALs)—whose unlocking enables unit commanders to use the proper numerical firing code.[15]

The whole C^3 system is worthless if it cannot survive the first stage of a nuclear exchange. Five challenges exist to C^3 survivability: physical destruction, particularly as warhead accuracy improves; electromagnetic pulses (EMP) produced by nuclear explosions capable of fouling up exposed electronic equipment; ionospheric disruption; jamming by enemy action; and antisatellite weaponry able to punch out the eyes and ears of military intelligence.[16] A major effort is underway to deal with these problems.

The National Military Command System (NMCS) consists basically of the NMCC, NORAD, and SAC, backed up by aircraft. It provides for alternative command posts for the president and defense chiefs, plus SAC's always-airborne command post code-named "Looking Glass." At some point in a potential nuclear crisis the president would be evacuated by helicopter from the White House south lawn and flown to Grisson Air Force Base in Indiana. There he boards "Kneecap"—the National Emergency Airborne Command Post (NEACP)—from which he would direct countermoves through telephone, teletype circuits, and all-frequency radio communication linking him to the specified and unified commands and services plus land and sea-based terminals. (The alternative NMCC near Fort Ritchie, Maryland, reportedly has the same capabilities.[17])

One of the potential weaknesses of the C³ system has been its major reliance on the Bell system, good as that is, for the bulk of telephonic communications. In the early 1980s 94% of the U.S. government's most critical communications circuits were leased from commercial carriers.[18] C³ upgrading aims at hardening of landlines and satellite ground stations, plus Extremely Low Frequency for improved conversations with submerged submarines, Very Low Frequency reception for bombers, and, further off, laser communication.

Antisatellite weaponry poses an obvious threat to C³. Today the ASATs on both sides can attack only reconnaissance and ELINT (electronic intelligence) satellites, with early-warning and communications satellites in still-unreachable geosynchronous orbits. Decreasing warning time has prompted development of NAVSTAR tracking satellites whose output would go directly to SAC, NORAD, and the NMCC.[19]

U.S. reluctance to ban ASAT testing is based in part on concern that Soviet surveillance satellites could one day make the oceans transparent to Soviet sensors, precisely targeting U.S. ships and submarines. But logically an ASAT ban would favor the United States, whose worldwide U.S. military C³ system is even more dependent on satellites not being knocked out. In terms of crisis stability, in a period of all-out ASAT competition a reported satellite failure in an intense crisis, accidental or not, might be taken as a signal of impending attack.

There is a more positive reason for keeping satellites off limits to weaponeers on both sides. As vividly demonstrated by one professional-level "wargame" conducted at MIT for the U.S. Navy, unhampered satellite observation could be crucial not just for military purposes, but for arms control and ceasefire purposes (in that particular case, high-speed surfacing and counting of submarines to ressure both sides that an attack was not in preparation).[20]

The Washington-Moscow hot line established in 1963[21] could be vital in enabling civilian leaders to collaborate to end a nuclear exchange before it ends them. Originally the hot line consisted of two telegraph and teleprinter terminals with duplex telegraph and radio telegraph circuits running via London-Copenhagen-Stockholm-Helsinki. It has reportedly been used, chiefly for purposes of mutual reassurance, on tense occasions such as the June 1967 Middle East War, the 1971 Indo-Pakistan War, the U.S.-Soviet confrontation that suddenly erupted during the 1973 Mideast War, and several times since. After it was accidentally cut by a Finnish farmer's plow, two additional circuits were added in 1971, this time using communication satellite transponders, U.S. and Soviet ground stations, and a radiotelegraph line running via Tangier.

Even during a period of tension, a further agreement was reached in July 1984, to upgrade the hot line to enable a speed-up from 64 to 192 words per minute and transmission of graphics including charts, maps, and drawings. While retaining the old teleprinters and high-speed facsimile lines, pictures will soon enjoy state-of-the-art resolution, and it will take less than two minutes to transmit two pages of text. The American terminal will continue to be located in the Pentagon, linked to the White House.[22] Reportedly, it was decided not to add voice or video capabilities to minimize emotionalism.

It must be added, however, that some analysts consider the C³ upgrading effort not only futile, but likely to strengthen the trend toward automated annihilation. One expert argues that a moderately small Soviet effort (50–100 warheads) sufficient to shatter U.S. linkages with its own strategic forces fits in with Soviet military doctrine, and concludes that ". . . there can be no possibility of controlling a nuclear war."[23] Another favors improvements in C³ but worries that with short warning times, decapitation doctrines, and possible delegation of release authority down the line as the alert level rises, more warning may bring less rather than more stability to crisis management by making political direction of a nuclear war virtually impossible.[24]

Possible confirmation of that concern comes from the memoirs of a recent White House official responsible for presidential nuclear strike orders and emergency evacuation sites. His conclusion was that "the system is a shambles":

The system is brilliantly conceived and executed from the detection networks around the world to the high-IQ computers at NORAD. But then, when it gets to the White House, it's all mashed potatoes. . . . If the crunch came, nothing would happen. . . . There isn't a hope in hell that [the president] is going to get on a conference call with his advisers before the mushroom clouds start forming. *Not once has the human failure factor been taken into account* [emphasis mine].[25]

There are, finally, slippages in the human chain that interprets commands from the top. An analysis of four major postwar crises shows how lower-level orders for alerts and deployments can seriously jeopardize the policy purposes of the top-level decision makers.[26]

It makes excellent sense to strengthen C³ to enable the nation's civilian leaders to maintain tight control over their nuclear forces in the face of ambiguous but worrisome indicators of possible attack, both to deter and to negotiate an end to the crisis. In the words of the head of the White House Communication Agency, ". . . a reliable command and control and communication system is a key issue in how not to let a war happen."[27]

But a system designed for worst cases must stand the test of worst cases, above all the human or "foul-up" factor. The problem is not that the emperor has no clothes. It is that in a real-life nuclear crisis there may be plenty of clothes but no emperor. The ultimate nightmare would find the national command authorities on one or both sides desperately wishing to terminate a potentially catastrophic exchange, while commanders who are cut off from headquarters fire off their nuclear weapons. Fictional scenarios about system malfunctions have harmlessly entertained us. But on mounting evidence, nature may come to imitate art. The corollary to Murphy's Law ("If anything can go wrong, it will") may one day be, "Murphy was an optimist."

The history of technology—including military technology—is riddled with unforeseen malfunctions. Complex systems sometimes fail, whether from equipment breakdown or "pilot error." At their most spectacular, they can generate a chain reaction of unplanned events in which the components of an interdependent system combine synergistically to produce ca-

lamitous results. Each part of the system has a low probability
of failing. But the ensuing cascade of events can add up to catastrophic system failure.

Notable instances of complex "fail-safe" mechanisms failing
are the great 1965 Northeast electric power blackout, previously considered technically inconceivable, and the massive
breakdown of the Three Mile Island nuclear power plant in
1979. Far graver were the catastrophic chemical leakage at the
Bhopal, India, Union Carbide plant in 1984 that caused more
than 2,500 deaths, the devastating explosion of a Soviet nuclear
reactor at Chernobyl the next year whose human toll is still
mounting, and the explosion of the U.S. shuttle *Challenger*. In
all these cases, crucial information was misinterpreted, mis-
judged, or ignored by ostensibly well-trained personnel. On the
military side, serious command and communication failures
produced an unplanned U-2 overflight of the Kola Peninsula
in the midst of the Cuban Missile Crisis of 1962, the 1968
North Korean seizure of the U.S.S. *Pueblo,* the more recent col-
lision of a Soviet nuclear submarine with a U.S. aircraft carrier
and near-miss of a Soviet carrier with a U.S. frigate, the probable Soviet mistaking of Korean Airline flight 007 for an intelligence-gathering intruder in 1983, resulting in their taking
269 innocent lives, and the wayward Soviet naval drone missile
that landed in Finland in 1985.

The favorite historic analogy to a war no one wants is the
chain of events in which the assassination in 1914 of Archduke
Ferdinand by Serbian nationalists led to the bloodbath of
World War I. Indeed, President John F. Kennedy, having read
The Guns of August not long before the Cuban Missile Crisis, is
reported to have said at the peak of the crisis that he did not
want anyone to have to write a book called *The Missiles of
October.*[28]

Reluctant guarantees, reciprocal mobilization, the final ulti-
matum—all were avoidable steps in a slide toward a disastrous
war from what today we would call a "local conflict." The degree to which that sequence was devoid of rational calculations
is caught in the question German Chancellor von Bülow asked
his successor—"How did it all happen?"—and the answer—
"Ah, if we only knew."

What particularly links the World War I tragedy to the contemporary situation is the primacy in both instances of offensive military doctrines and strategies. According to historian

Barbara Tuchman, the very nature of Germany's Schlieffen Plan pressured civilian leaders to make hasty and aggressive decisions:

Suddenly dismayed—(they) struggled and twisted to fend it off. It was of no use. . . . General Staffs, goaded by their relentless time-tables, were pounding the table for the signal to move lest their opponents gain an hour's head start. Appalled upon the brink, the chiefs of state who would be ultimately responsible for their country's fate attempted to back away but the pull of military schedules dragged them forward.[29]

Some argue that such cases of malfunction in crisis are not really analogous, armed as we are with historical knowledge, the special rationality fostered by the unthinkability of nuclear holocaust, and an efficient C^3 system. Perhaps it will still be technically possible to maintain control at times of unprecedented tension. But what of the human factor?

The potential Achilles heel in crisis planning resides in the assumptions it makes, often unconsciously, about human beings who must carry out the plans. Military training is designed to drill procedures into human consciousness until they are ingrained and can be relied on under pressure. But plans for national crisis management at the highest level rarely consider the human factor, focusing instead on technological solutions. The trouble is, the "engineering blueprints" imply Herculean demands on humans as well as on machines.

Which brings us to the constant on the right-hand side of our earlier equation: the human component of nuclear crisis management.

The Human Side of the Crisis Equation

It is common knowledge that foreign policy crises are stressful. Historians have amply demonstrated that foreign policy decision making under intense strain can produce distorted results. Well-known examples are American leaders blocking out signals of impending attacks on Pearl Harbor in 1941 and South Korea in 1950, and Joseph Stalin stubbornly denying mounting evidence of a probable Nazi attack (and, according to Nikita Khrushchev, going into a catatonic seizure on hearing it had taken place).

Some officials at the apex of the national security apparatus confess to thriving on crises. A magisterial celebration of this phenomenon comes from Henry A. Kissinger, who said of his White House service,

Periods of crisis, to be sure, involve great tension, but they are also characterized by a strange tranquility. . . . Personality clashes are reduced. . . . In a crisis only the strongest strive for responsibility . . . the few prepared to grapple with circumstances are usually undisturbed in the eye of a hurricane . . . they themselves operate in . . . a great stillness that yields, as resolution nears, to exhaustion, exhilaration or despair.[30]

Robert Kennedy later wrote of the Cuban Missile Crisis, "That kind of pressure does strange things to a human being. . . . For some it brings out characteristics and strengths that perhaps even they never knew they had, and for others, the pressure is too overwhelming."[31]

I can attest to the unearthly sangfroid of some of the highest officials of government who register intense stimulation from crisis, and profound boredom when "nothing is happening." I happen to believe that this species of chronic crisis mentality distorts the foreign policy agenda and lessens the chances for thoughtful policy planning.[32] But in fairness, crisis researchers have good evidence that decision makers under stress usually make a greater effort to behave rationally, and in that sense crises can be positively beneficial. Indeed, social scientists have long observed that mild stress facilitates decision making and even improves its quality.

But the same researchers of stress also observe an inverted U-shaped curve along which "every individual reaches a 'threshold' or crossover point (leading to) rapid decline in performance."[33] That "decline in performance" translates into a numbing litany of individual and organizational malfunctions catalogued by studies of stress. Some of the relevant malfunctions, along with well-known coping mechanisms that distort objective reality:

• increased rigidity leading to intolerance of ambiguity and fixation on one alternative,

• defensive/avoidance mechanisms such as bolstering, denial, procrastination, and withdrawal,

• alternatively: illusions of invulnerability, belligerence, and aggressiveness,

• collapsed time perspective and neglect of future consequences,

• unquestioned belief in the group's moral superiority, and tendency to consult only with those in agreement,

• stereotyping of opponents, resulting in self-fulfilling prophecies,

• worst-case analysis (usually replacing earlier best-case analysis),

• information overload and improper information handling, including poor search methods and selective bias,

• suppression of personal doubts, creating illusion of unanimity,

• failure to implement decisions due to their complexity,

• confusion due to organizational bottlenecks,

• rigid and inflexible standard operating procedures (SOPs),

• narrowing options and incomplete consideration (or reconsideration) of alternatives,

• failure to examine risks of preferred choices or to make contingency plans,

• reliance on inappropriate historical analogies and lessons,

• employment of misleading mirror-image mechanisms,

• declining sense of responsibility for outcomes,

• hypervigilance characteristic of a panic state,

• demoralization.

A particular set of problems arises for the *group* decision making common in foreign affairs. Students of behavior identify a pervasive tendency to distort objective reality through a mechanism Irving Janis christened "groupthink." Members of any small cohesive group tend to sustain esprit de corps by unconsciously rejecting dissenting views, while developing shared illusions that interfere with critical thinking.[34]

But the heart of the matter lies in clinically observed impairments of *individual* performance under stress. The decision-maker's "psychological world" is defined as his or her accumulated "cluster of ideas, beliefs, values, personality characteristics. . . ."[35] When people confront a crisis, even before fatigue sets in they bring it to their particular mind-sets— "cognitive maps"—and strive, consciously or not, to accommodate new information to their belief structures. One survey of cases finds overwhelming evidence that decision makers "fit incoming information into their existing theories and images" and "tend to perceive what they expect."[36] The more intense the crisis, the more the individual hunkers down into his or her ingrained patterns of behavior and belief, moving toward what psychologists call cognitive rigidity.

One consequence of this all-too-human trait is failure to understand what the other side is trying to communicate, particularly when the signals are subtle. Another review of historic cases reveals that, while people "flatter themselves by thinking that they search for subtle and elusive clues to others' behavior," their messages "not only convey different meanings to each side, but each is usually unaware of the discrepancy." The result is chronic underestimation of the "degree to which the other side's policies are the product of internal bargaining, internal misunderstandings, or subordinates not following instructions. . . ."[37] A review of twenty-four professional-level American political-military crisis simulations observed a "severe inability by the United States to understand the expressed intentions of another state."[38] A former high defense official writes that policymakers "hear what they want to hear."[39] (All of the above also makes the increasingly unrealistic assumption of a drug-free bureaucracy.)

I have emphasized the threat to rational decision making of excessively *short* decision times. Students of the Cuban Missile Crisis believe that if the decision had been forced within 48 hours instead of a week, it would have taken the form of a military attack on Cuba, with incalculable consequences.[40] But at the other extreme we can worry about the behavior of individuals *too long* under stress, who are literally exhausted. *The fatigue factor is one of the most important yet least understood aspects of crisis decision making.* A former White House staffer described the "paramount role of executive fatigue" among top officials who "make bad policy and then compound it."[41] Presidential Assistant Theodore Sorensen "saw first-hand . . . how brutally physical and mental fatigue can numb the good sense as well as the senses of normally articulate men."[42]

Veterans of foreign policy crises sometimes boast of having gone without sleep for days on end of unremitting tensions, punctuated only by catnaps and infusions of caffeine. But experimental evidence demonstrates "that human beings cannot tolerate long periods of sleep deprivation without experiencing significant behavioral modification." And a startling perspective on Hot Line communications in two widely separated time zones is opened up by the possibility that "bargaining behavior . . . could very well be affected by . . . diurnal cycles and circadian rhythms."[43]

In an age of accurate guidance and doctrines of political decapitation, the already oppressive strains on decision makers in a full-blown crisis will be magnified by a sense of *personal threat*. Even in nonnuclear crises, Margaret Hermann observed that where personal threat was felt, "the policymaker becomes emotionally aroused, experiencing such feelings as distress, fear, uncertainty, or anxiety."[44] Everyone who has served within the crisis machine or watched momentous announcements on television has seen the symptoms of visible distress: flustered or speeded-up speech, perspiration, altered voice quality, bodily tension. Such feelings were reported by more than one member of President Kennedy's executive committee ("ExCom") that managed the Cuban Missile Crisis, and have been publicly displayed by more than one president and secretary of state.

Researchers of disaster behavior have reported that the greater the perceived danger, the smaller the percentage of individuals "who make full use of the available information and choose an effective course of action." Ironic considering the enormous attention currently given to improved warning is their conclusion that "when people are warned about incoming danger that will materialize within a very short time interval, their fear mounts to such a high level and they act so inappropriately that they would be better off with no warning at all."[45]

In U.S. defense arrangements a vast effort has gone into the Personnel Reliability System for screening military personnel to "ensure their stability, reliability, and suitability" before allowing them near nuclear weapons.[46] But no comparable screening exists of the president, his cabinet officers or national security advisers. Perhaps political leaders and senior bureaucrats are sufficiently tougher than the rest of humanity to be exempt from the medical conclusion that chronic stress "overtaxes the body's stamina and may lead to nervous and physical breakdowns and finally to death."[47]

But maybe not.

Making It Through the Twentieth Century, or What to Do Till the Doctor Comes

Strategic policy is no exception to the rule that large systems can usually be reformed only at the margins. The theoretical possibility of global disaster has been with us for decades. Negotiated agreements can reduce the number of weapons, and even contemplate their eventual abolition.

There will still be major crises in a world of turbulent change, and it remains essential to grasp the logical implications of new accuracies, deployments, and strategic doctrines that will make it less possible than before to wait out ambiguities and uncertainties in crises, regardless of the numbers of nuclear weapons. Nor, after examining the data, are we entitled to have unbroken confidence in human rationality in highly stressed individuals who make portentous judgments under intimidating conditions.

One remedial step Americans (and hopefully Soviets) are taking is to upgrade the technology of C[3] so that even under desperate circumstances, decision makers can maintain contact with their nuclear forces and with each other. But some current "fixes" carry their own perverse dilemmas. For example, safe alternative command posts are essential for effective C[3]. Yet in a tense crisis, evacuation of civilian leadership, like evacuation of city populations, is a signal the other side must unavoidably read as an indication of possible attack. If precautionary evacuation of the president is undesirable,[48] and given the impossibility in a worst case of evaluating complex data and making rational decisions in a handful of minutes, only three alternatives logically present themselves.

One is to decentralize to local military commands early in a crisis the authority to launch nuclear weapons. If the United States is actually under attack, it could be certain to retaliate; more to the point, the decentralized ability to do so would presumably strengthen deterrence. But in the likelier case of a false alarm generating ambiguous indicators and mutually escalatory alerts, such loss of civilian control would be intolerable.

A second alternative is to program computers to order launch of retaliatory forces on the basis of preprogrammed indicators. If the problem were a clear-cut Soviet assault, a kind of "doomsday machine" that launches under attack might be convincing evidence that reprisal is guaranteed without waiting for fatigued, panicked or defunct human decision makers. But for the likelier scenarios, the accumulating history of system malfunctions should decisively rule out the highly dubious doctrine of "launch on warning."

It is difficult to avoid the logical conclusion that the nuclear crisis decision-making system simply cannot be expected to work as planned without major alterations in both weaponry and strategic doctrines, plus purposeful measures to offset the hazards of human malfunction.

In concrete terms, this third alternative calls for steps to return the weapons, the strategies and the deployments to the earlier relative stability that gave civilian decision makers confidence they could ride out crises, wait for confirmation or reassurance, and meanwhile conduct deescalatory diplomacy. The following recommendations are for the most part not new. But they flow directly from the logic of the foregoing analysis.

• Two questions should constitute the acid test for making policy choices about strategy: First, "Does this weapon/policy/strategy/procedure give civilian leadership time to be clear what is happening in a nuclear crisis before making fateful decisions?" And second, "Are adequate precautions taken to ensure maximum rationality on the part of highly stressed decision makers?"

• Any plans for "decapitation" of the other side's civilian decision-making centers should be forgone. Concretely, this calls for seeking agreement to reduce or eliminate systems that put the other side on a "hair-trigger," whether Soviet offshore submarine patrols and depressed trajectory missiles that threaten Washington, or missiles in Western Europe that can dig out Soviet command centers in minutes.

• To meet the same test, strategic doctrines should minimize reliance on early nuclear use under any contingency save confirmed direct nuclear attack. By diplomacy or by example, urgent steps should be taken to substitute dispersed, mobile "Midgetman" types of single-warhead missiles for "all-eggs-in-one-basket" heavily MIRVed systems such as Soviet SS-18s and the U.S. MX, and to reinforce existing agreements not to hide strategic delivery systems from external verification.

• At least in theory, an effective strategic weapons *defense* could permit the nuclear superpowers to conduct their adversarial relationship without mutual survival being put at risk. In addition to its moral superiority to a potentially genocidal policy of threatened massive retaliation, a defensive world should be at least as crisis-stable as the retaliation-dominated one we have learned to live with. But paradoxically, the *process* of seeking safety through antimissile defenses could produce the most unstable world of all. The most perilous moment in the U.S.-Soviet relationship could occur during a crisis at a time when one superpower seemed to be beating the other to a relatively effective missile defense.

• Actual evidence about the consequences of such asymmetries is mercifully scarce. But in at least one high-level governmental crisis exercise, one side, fearing that the other believed its silos sufficiently protected against retaliation to do the unthinkable, was irresistibly pressured to strike preemptively—and suicidally. Defense Secretary Weinberger unwittingly confirmed the point when in December 1983 he called *Soviet* development of an effective ballistic missile defense "one of the most frightening prospects I could imagine."[49] To preserve stability, the framework for developing antimissile defenses cannot be other than through a parallel or even joint, rather than unilateral, effort, however daunting the obstacles to doing so.

• Negotiated agreements banning or limiting antisatellite weaponry testing and deployment in outer space would retain the essential C^3 on which we rely, as well as reducing the chance that a technological malfunction will automatically be misread as a threatening indicator. The 1967 Outer Space Treaty should be supplemented with new "rules of the road" concerning behavior under changing conditions in outer space.[50]

• For crisis deescalation purposes in cases of third-party mischief or ambiguous superpower actions, the Hot Line should be supplemented with additional means for exchanging data and reassurances so as to avoid misunderstandings. One promising route lies in proposals now on the table for "crisis reduction centers" in the two capitals as well as in a neutral area.[51]

• Along with military policies, future crisis stability requires actions in the political-diplomatic realm. Great power "spheres of influence" once helped avoid war, but today are unfashionably imperialistic. American and Soviet leaders could, however, hold discussions on what might be called "Spheres of *Abstention*,"[52] identifying regional conflict situations both should by now have learned it is in their mutual self-interest to insulate from external meddling, exploiting the potential of a U.N. or other mutilateral umbrella rather than, as in the past, first taking the go-it-alone route.

• Psychologists have long urged monitoring for irrational behavior at the top. Such recommendations sometimes call for obtrusive or insulting procedures, and in any event those elected or appointed to high office seldom admit the possibility of irrationality. But trained psychiatrists do monitor lower command levels for pathological effects of fatigue and excess stress among pilots, submariners, and missile officers. It is obviously more important to do the same at the apex of the decision-making pyramid. A psychologically trained individual should be assigned as an inner circle "damage control officer" to watch for symptoms of irrational behavior and alert officials accordingly.

• If junior officers in underground missile control centers and aboard ship are required, as a safeguard against individual pathology, to share the responsibility for firing their weapons, it is far more important to do so where the stakes are infinitely greater. An additional safeguard would be a "two-key" procedure for the president and his designated surrogates in the descending national command authorities chain.

• National decision making is grounded in the perceptions leaders have in their minds concerning the behavior of the other side. In fact, of all impairments of foreign policy decision making, the most costly arise from mutual misperceptions. Enough evidence exists of a profound cultural gulf between Soviets and Americans to warrant building into the top-level decision system better means of assessing the other side's actions, signals and intentions. A proven device for overcoming official cultural ignorance is political gaming.[53] But it is necessary to involve not just lower levels of the bureaucracy, but the president and his closest political advisers in simulations with competent experts, in which their built-in conceptions and expectations about Soviet reactions are pretested before crises occur.

Can history be rolled back in this way? Is not the march of technology inexorable? The rational answer is that no impersonal force ordained that each nuclear superpower strive to improve its own ability to keep control and communicate in crises, while simultaneously working to blind, deafen and decapitate the other. The maintenance of "crisis-stability," with whatever policy actions that takes, should be the highest priority on the agenda of national security.

Afterword: Rethinking National Security and Arms Control
Dean Rusk

There is a very special quality about our relations with the Soviet Union. We are the only two nations who, if locked in mortal conflict, could raise a serious question about whether this planet could sustain the human race. That imposes upon the two of us a massive common responsibility.

In the field of arms control we and they have an obligation in the nuclear nonproliferation treaty to make a serious effort to find some way to put limits on nuclear weapons and to reduce them. We also begin with the notion that we and the Soviet Union have a fundamental common interest in avoiding nuclear war. Leaders on both sides know that.

In this postwar period public opinion, informed by news media and politicians, tends to swing like a pendulum back and forth between détente and the cold war. However, it is not really an either-or question. Elements of détente and the cold war have been simultaneous parts of our relations with the Soviet Union since World War II. To me the word détente means little more than a continuing, persistent, serious effort to find points of agreement on large matters or small. That effort helps to broaden our base of common interests and reduce the range of issues on which violence might occur.

It did not begin in the early 1970s when a lot was being said about détente. It began immediately after World War II. Most people have forgotten that in 1946 the United States, the United Kingdom, and Canada went into the United Nations with a plan called the Baruch Plan, under which all fissionable materials would be turned over to the United Nations to be used solely for peaceful purposes. There were to be no nuclear weapons in the hands of any nation, including ourselves. Unfortunately, we could not get the Soviets to negotiate seriously on that latter point. Lest I appear to patronize them on this point, let me simply say that if the Soviet Union had been the first to develop the atomic bomb and had made exactly the same proposals in the United Nations as we did, before we ourselves had the know-how, I cannot honestly say the then executive and legislative branches of our government would have accepted the proposal. Nevertheless there was a fleeting moment in time when a great opportunity was lost. From that time forward, so long as the human race shall exist, its chief problem will be to keep the nuclear beast in its cage.

Shortly after that, President Truman and Secretary of State Marshall invited the Soviet Union and other countries to participate in the Marshall Plan. The Soviet Union walked out of the European meeting where governments consulted together about how they would respond to the invitation. And when they walked out, they dragged a very reluctant Czechoslovakia and Poland with them. Again, I am not being sanctimonious. Had the Soviets been a major participant in the Marshall Plan, I think it is clear we would have had very considerable difficulty in getting the necessary appropriations from Congress.

During the Eisenhower administration, after literally hundreds of negotiating sessions, we achieved the Austrian State Treaty, which led to the withdrawal of all occupying forces from that fine little country and allowed it to move into the future as an independent, neutral country. And, during those same years, we achieved a brilliant piece of preventive diplomacy. All national claims in the Antarctic were put in cold storage. The entire area was barred from military operations and activities. It was reserved for scientific research, and arrangements were made for us to visit each other's installations regularly, to assure ourselves that the treaty was being complied with.

After grievous crises over Berlin and the Cuban missiles, President Kennedy, Vice-President Johnson, and their senior colleagues concluded it was just too late in history for the two nuclear superpowers to pursue a policy of total hostility across the board. So, despite those crises, they set in motion the process that produced the Nuclear Test Ban Treaty of 1963, a civil air agreement providing for flights between New York and Moscow, a consular agreement that has made it somewhat easier for us to give effective protection for Americans traveling or working in the Soviet Union, two important space treaties, the first part of an agreement on the nonproliferation of nuclear weapons, and the beginnings of talks on the antiballistic missile treaty.

Those efforts were continued into the Nixon administration. In that period the ABM treaty and the nonproliferation treaty were concluded, as well as a very useful, new four-power agreement on Berlin, which has reduced the role of that city as a flash point of violence among the great powers.

I should say at this point that as far as I can see into the future, the Russians are not going to trust us and we are not going to trust the Russians. But that does not mean we cannot have effective agreements. For example, if the Soviets had not treated our planes flying into Moscow properly, we could have taken action against Aeroflot planes coming into New York. Their credit on Wall Street is good because they pay their commercial bills. If they stop doing that, their credit will drop to zero. We do not have to sit around growing ulcers about whether they are complying with the Nuclear Test Ban Treaty of '63, because if they were to explode nuclear weapons in the atmosphere or underwater or in outer space, our government would know about it immediately and then consider what steps, if any, needed to be taken. There are ways to make agreements based on what generally is called verification, which can be effective among those who do not trust each other. When I go into a bank to make a deposit, I do not ask myself whether the teller is honest. Because we have bank examiners and the Federal Deposit Insurance Corporation the question of trust does not even arise.

Trust based on verification is one thread in our relations with the Soviet Union in this postwar period. On the other hand there is a thread of repeated confrontations with them. Most of us learned in school and college the sad story of what happened during the 1930s, when the weakness, pacifism, and isolationist sentiments of democracies led my generation of students into the catastrophe of a World War II, which could have been prevented.

On the other hand, most of us have forgotten what happened just after V-J Day. We demobilized almost completely overnight. By the summer of 1946 we did not have a single division in our army or a single group in our air force that could be considered ready for combat. The ships of our navy were being put into mothballs almost as fast as we could find berths for them, and those that remained afloat were being manned by skeleton crews. It is a matter of public record that our defense budget for three fiscal years, '47, '48, and '49, was slightly over $11 billion a year.

As Mr. Stalin looked out across the west he saw all the divisions melting away. So what did he do? He gave the U.N. Security Council its first case by trying to keep his forces in Azerbaijan, the northwest province of Iran. He demanded possession of the two eastern provinces of Turkey, Kars and Ardahan, and a share in the control of the straits leading into the Black Sea. He ignored the wartime agreements giving the people of Eastern Europe some real say in their own political future. He supported sanctuaries in places like Albania, Yugoslavia, and Bulgaria for the guerrillas going after Greece. He had a hand in the Communist coup d'etat in Czechoslovakia. He blockaded Berlin. He gave the green light to the North Koreans to go after South Korea. The revisionist historians can write until all the ink runs dry, but those were the events that started the cold war.

We were disarmed. It was not until 1950 that we began to build up our armed forces in any significant way.

In sum, we have had a series of severe differences, some of them very dangerous, with the Soviet Union. They began with those events I just mentioned, to which were added confrontations in Korea, Southeast Asia, Berlin, Cuba, and Afghanistan; marches into the countries of Eastern Europe; pressure on Poland; and so forth. We have lived together through a very rough-and-tumble experience.

There are times when these problems of confrontation get in the way of the search for agreement. While I dislike linking one particular problem with all the other problems, because the total is too large to manage in any single discussion or negotiation, nevertheless some of these things do get linked. For example, on a certain Wednesday morning in August 1968, we and the Russians were set to make an identical, simultaneous announcement in Washington and Moscow that President Lyndon Johnson would shortly go to Leningrad to open what later came to be known as the SALT Talks. The trouble is, on the very night before the announcement, Soviet forces marched into Czechoslovakia. I had to telephone the Soviet ambassador in Washington to insist he phone Moscow and tell the Soviets not to make that joint announcement the next morning. Ironically, several years later, any chance of getting Senate approval of the SALT II Treaty was destroyed when Soviet forces marched into Afghanistan.

I have young people in mind when I make my next observation. I am concerned that they are being battered on all sides by talk of Doomsday. I know from my experience as well as from reports from different parts of the country that this Doomsday talk is having a significant and negative impact upon them. An important thing to remember is that by August 9, 1986, the anniversary of the dropping of the second atomic bomb on Nagasaki, we had put behind us 41 years since a nuclear weapon had been fired in anger. Some limits have been observed by both the United States and the U.S.S.R. in our difficult and stormy relationship. I have not found anyone who is saying that to these young people.

I think we have learned two quite important things during these 41 years. One is that the fingers on the nuclear trigger are not itchy. Indeed, in support of collective security, the American people have taken something like 600,000 casualties in dead and wounded since the end of World War II, without the firing of nuclear weapons. While that is a terrible toll to me, it is also a solid demonstration that at least the American fingers on that trigger are not itchy. And, I think we also have learned that Soviet leaders have no more interest in destroying Mother Russia than our leaders have in destroying our beloved United States. We can build on that.

Of course, that is no solid guarantee for the future. We do have to be careful. We and the Russians came out of the Cuban Missile Crisis with a sense that we had better try to avoid such crises because they are just too utterly dangerous. I am not sure whether that prudence will be passed successfully from hand to hand as leaders succeed leaders. I think we ought to have learned we should not play games of chicken with each other, to see how far we can go in pressing points of view or taking actions without crossing that fatal line.

I think we also ought to watch the level of rhetoric between the two sides. When it becomes too high and too vitriolic there is always the possibility that one side or the other might begin to believe its own rhetoric. President Lyndon Johnson would not let those of us in his administration criticize any foreign leader by name, whether it was Khrushchev or de Gaulle or Mao Tse-tung. His view was that that is simply not the way to solve problems.

While we do have to be careful, I do not believe we should think about these problems in an atmosphere of panic or of gloom and doom, because that would get in the way of sober, positive, and constructive thinking.

Where does that leave us? We and the Soviets have an almost infinitely large potential agenda in our discussions with each other. In our relationships with them, on small matters or large, we should try to act on the basis of the best that is in us. One of the reasons Harry Truman was a great president is that he had great confidence in the grass roots of the American people. He really did believe that the American people at their best were a very good people and would do what had to be done at the end of the day if they understood what it was and why.

However, we are not always at our best. Sometimes we find ourselves acting in a way that is beneath our own dignity and not consonant with our own approach to life. For example, during the 1960s I asked Ambassador Dobrynin to come to see me through the basement door of the State Department and to use my private elevator so we could talk without having swarms of reporters from all over town trying to find out what he was there to talk about. But, early in the Reagan administration it was decided the Soviet ambassador should come to the main diplomatic entrance where everybody else comes. Instead of giving him a phone call ahead of time and asking him to come to the diplomatic entrance, they had television and newspaper reporters out there waiting for him to try to enter through the basement door, only to be halted and backed up unceremoniously and then be shoved around to the other entrance. That just was not necessary.

I shared everyone's horror and dismay at the extraordinary tragedy of the shooting down of the Korean Airline plane. But, I thought it was not in accordance with our own character for us to say to Mr. Gromyko, If you want to come to the United Nations General Assembly, you have to land at a military airfield. We know he could not accept that. Mr. Gromyko, in one capacity or another, has served alongside nine American presidents and fourteen secretaries of state. We have a treaty obligation to facilitate delegates' access to the United Nations. It would, I think, have been better for us simply to allow him to come to the United Nations General Assembly in the usual fashion.

We do have to recognize, however, that negotiating with the Russians is a very difficult matter. Cemeteries are filled with tombstones of those who have come to Washington beating their breasts saying, I know how to deal with the Russians. It *is* difficult to deal with the Russians. They take a conspiratorial approach to politics even in their relations among themselves. And there are times when we use the same words, but they simply do not convey the same meanings. During the 1970s, when Mr. Nixon and Mr. Kissinger were talking so much about détente, the Soviets were talking among themselves about peaceful coexistence. To them, peaceful coexistence apparently means a continuation of the struggle by all means short of general war. This is hardly a synonym for what we mean when we use the word détente.

It has taken us a long time to get their leaders to become reasonably familiar with this extraordinarily complicated constitutional system of ours, perhaps the most complicated one in the world. I have spent a lot of my personal time with them trying to educate them a bit on this strange system we have. I think they finally know that if the president agrees with them on something and the Congress refuses to approve, it is not necessarily bad faith on the part of the president. And, I think they have finally concluded that the *New York Times* is not the official spokesman for the U.S. government.

It is inevitable that they, living where they live, with problems that are somewhat different from ours, look upon some of the common issues we have with them from a different point of view.

One of the most urgent tasks we have is to try to find a way to put some limits on this otherwise insane arms race, but when you talk to them bilaterally about it there are some ghosts at the table. For example, the ghost of the People's Republic of China, a billion Chinese armed with nuclear weapons with whom they share a common frontier of several thousands of miles. At times, although they do not put it in these terms, whatever seems to us a reasonable balance between the Soviet Union and the United States will not work. They want something extra because of China. I have no doubt they are also concerned about the increasing range of British and French nuclear weapons. It is not unreasonable for them to have that concern. A more difficult problem is their resistance to effective verification, partly because they do not need verification measures from us. We are asking them for what amounts to a unilateral concession. When they look at us, they see an open society, where in many places they can drive down county roads and make triangulations of missile sites, or read technical journals. We are a government that does not know how to keep its mouth shut, and adding a little dose of espionage to that, the Soviets can get what information they need about us.

When we look at them, however, we see large areas of the country that are closed. We see a government that really does know how to keep its mouth shut and a place where espionage in the usual sense is very difficult to maintain. So, it is not easy for them to accept the straightforward, all-out measures of verification that would make arms agreements possible.

The arms race is a book with many different chapters in it. It is not a single problem. The Soviet Union occasionally digs up some of the oldest diplomatic maneuvers in anyone's bargaining kit—such as trying to charge us a price of admission just to get the other side to the negotiation table.

For example, the Soviet negotiators long ago suggested talks to prevent the arms race from moving into outer space. We came back saying as a precondition we wanted to talk about missiles they had earlier refused to discuss. By the time we got around to withdrawing that precondition, they came up with one, namely, that we would have to agree to abandon our testing of antisatellite weapons while the negotiations were going on. We really ought to stop dancing that kind of minuet on both sides. We should forget about the games and get down to serious discussion of matters on their own merits.

I doubt very much that it will be possible to achieve a comprehensive arms limitation agreement. But it should be possible to separate out some elements of it and move on those and not wait until we can get every item tied together. For example, it seems to me we can separate out the problem of allowing the arms race to move into outer space. There are already existing treaties that seem to point in the other direction, the space treaties and the Anti-Ballistic Missile Treaty. Furthermore, we know we are talking about hundreds of billions of dollars to achieve any such weapon system. The Pentagon has already given testimony to the Congress that the development and deployment of lasers, x-ray lasers, and particle beam weapons in space would be comparable to ten times the effort that went into the Manhattan Project to build the atomic bomb.

We must also accept the fact that whatever we can do in this field, the Russians can do. The idea that we might somehow achieve an ultimate advantage over them in such matters seems to me to be patently ridiculous. We regularly underestimated their capabilities to develop things such as the atomic bomb, the hydrogen bomb, the first object in space, the first manned space flight. Just as certain as the rising of the sun is the fact that if we or the Soviet Union begins to move toward the scientific and technical capacity for placing weapons in space, we shall then be asked for additional hundreds of billions of dollars to build offensive weapons to penetrate or evade these esoteric defenses.

At the end of the 1960s and the early 1970s, we and the Soviets looked at this problem very carefully. The two of us agreed, with respect to the Anti-Ballistic Missile Treaty, that if we began to build up our defensive missiles on both sides, that would simply cause each side to multiply its offensive missiles in order to smother or penetrate the ABMs. So in the early Nixon years, we concluded the treaty that limits us to one array on each side. The prospect is that if we go down this trail again, we shall spend something in the range of a trillion dollars without any significant change in the underlying strategic relationship between the United States and the Soviet Union.

Any fourth grade schoolchild confronted with these facts would say, Well, then, why take that journey if you can find some way to prevent it? I would hope very much that we and the Soviets can sit down seriously to find ways to prevent the arms race from moving into outer space. We have done it in Antarctica. We have done it with the deployment of nuclear weapons on the deep sea ocean bed, and we thought we had done it thus far in outer space. So, we should make the effort.

I concluded some testimony before a committee of Congress by saying I hoped that my grandchildren would be able to look up into the vast universe and reflect with the Psalmist that the heavens declare the glory of God, not the folly of man.

There are many other matters on our agenda. We ought to approach the Soviet Union across a broad front. I could recite a litany of Soviet misdeeds in this postwar period that would raise your anger level several degrees. But, anger standing alone has no future. Whatever we think of the Russians or they think of us, we and they must still find some way to inhabit this speck of dust in the universe at the same time.

There is a very wide range of possibilities for finding points of agreement. Over the next 30 years, the entire human race is going to be faced with problems that are different in kind and in scale from those we have faced before and that will require some reasonable answers within a matter of decades if the human race is to avoid catastrophe.

I am thinking of the energy problem. At the moment our attitudes toward energy use would indicate we are still living in a fool's paradise. I am thinking of the impact of man's activities on the environment. We are in danger of inflicting irreparable damage upon this thin biosphere around the surface of the earth in which our species must live. Although there is some indication that some birth rates are coming down, I am thinking of the consequences of the population explosion. When I talk to my students, I am aware of the fact that before they get to be my age the prospect is that there will be between 10 and 15 billion people on this planet. These are some things that ought to bring us and the Soviet Union together simply because we are members of the same species. It would be useful in areas where we are not competitive in the stricter sense for us to find ways to put our heads together and make more sense out of the condition of man.

In the files of the State Department there is a letter from me dated a few years ago in which I suggest somebody have in the back of his mind that the time will come when we ought to be ready and willing to extend technical assistance to the Soviet Union in growing food. We are going to come into a period when everyone who can grow food must do it, because one of the oldest causes of war in the history of the human race, the pressure of people upon resources, is being revived in a world where there are thousands of megatons lying around in the hands of frail human beings. At present, this is not a workable idea, and I am sure some farmers in Minnesota would not care very much about that right now. But, if there is one thing we do know how to do in this country, it is to grow food. I think we can at some point take a major step in our own interest by finding ways to assist other countries, including the Soviet Union, in growing the food that is going to be essential for the prevention of war.

To use a military analogy, we should advance on these problems with the Soviet Union, like the advance of infantry on a broad front. We should move where we can. If cultural exchanges can encourage dialogue in other areas, we should engage in more of them. If we come across a problem that is more troublesome and resistant, we will have to take more time with it and work at it, perhaps work around it. I think we have no choice.

I have seen the Soviets in operation in this postwar period, sometimes very closely. They are not ten feet tall. They are human beings like the rest of us. They too have a basket of problems. They have problems with the other nationalities in their own system, with their youth, with various social ills, with the countries of Eastern Europe. There are many signs that the Eastern Europeans in the Soviet bloc harbor a strong nostalgic desire to be once again part of the great community of arts and sciences and letters and culture called Europe without any regard to differences between communism and capitalism.

The Soviets have some very serious problems with their economy. In regard to Afghanistan, I suggested to one Soviet friend that they invite me to Moscow to give them some technical assistance on how to get bogged down in a small country. I do not get much satisfaction out of recognizing they have serious problems, because there are moments when I think they must be more than a little frightened. That gives me no comfort. When people get frightened, they can become dangerous.

President Reagan at first had some special problems because of transitory leadership in the Soviet Union. During that kind of period, policymaking tends to sink into the bureaucracy, into such faceless people as the Secretariat of the Politburo, for example. And when that happens, you see some of the sociology of committees at work. A kind of inertia sets in. A kind of ideological orthodoxy becomes important. It was not easy for Mr. Reagan.

On our side, we must be sure that we get our own house in order. There have been some problems with that in recent years. We should remember the first sentence of Article II of the Constitution, "The Executive power shall be vested in a President of the United States of America." Only a president can clarify American policy on major issues when there are differences of view among the advisers around him.

So, we have some unfinished business. But, again, coming back to our young people, we should not destroy their sense of hope and confidence. We should give them a chance to build their own lives and not be unduly swept by the tides of passion that make sensible negotiations difficult.

Notes

Chapter 2 (The Use and Nonuse of Nuclear Weapons)

1. Seweryn Bailer, editor, *The Domestic Context of Soviet Foreign Policy* (Boulder, CO: Westview Press, 1981), p. 435.

2. Lawrence Freedman, *The Evolution of Nuclear Strategy* (St. Martin's Press, 1981), p. 399.

3. Committee of Soviet Scientists for Peace Against Nuclear Threat, *Space-Based Anti-Missile System with Directed Enemy Weapons: Strategic, Legal and Political Implications* (Moscow, 1984), pp. 30, 31, 32.

4. A report by the Union of Concerned Scientists, *Space-Based Missile Defense* (March 1984), pp. 5, 6.

5. Letter from Admiral Gayler to the author.

6. Robert Jervis, *The Illogic of American Nuclear Strategy* (Cornell University Press, 1984), p. 167.

7. Thomas Powers, "What Is It About?" *The Atlantic Monthly* (January 1984), p. 42.

8. Desmond Ball, "Can Nuclear War Be controlled?" *Adelphi Papers* #169 (International Institute for Strategic Studies, 1981), p. 37.

9. Robert S. McNamara, "The Military Role of Nuclear Weapons: Perceptions and Misperceptions," *Foreign Affairs* (Fall 1983), p. 72.

10. Desmond Ball, "Can Nuclear War Be Controlled?" *Adelphi Papers* #169 (International Institute for Strategic Studies, 1981), p. 38.

11. George F. Kennan, *The Nuclear Delusion—Soviet-American Relations in the Atomic Age* (New York: Pantheon Books), pp. 194–195.

12. For a brief summary of French strategic policy, see Lieut. General Charles Georges Fricaud-Chagnaud, "The French Defense," *Bulletin of the Atomic Scientists* (May 1984), p. 14.

13. Fricaud-Chagnaud. See note 12.

Chapter 3 (Arms Control: Old Debate, New Departures)

1. Two works that have stood the test of time in this field are Thomas Schelling and Morton Halperin, *Strategy and Arms Control* (New York: Twentieth

Century Fund, 1961), and Hedley Bull, *The Control of the Arms Race* (New York: Praeger, 1961).

2. By contrast the perspective of Secretary of Defense Robert McNamara in proposing an ABM ban in 1967 and of President Carter in negotiating the SALT II Treaty are more closely aligned with the classical objectives of arms control.

3. The Reagan administration's approach to arms control was laid out well before the 1980 election in Edward N. Luttwak, "Why Arm Control Has Failed," *Commentary* (January 1978), pp. 19–28. Numerous public statements by Secretary of Defense Weinberger expressing lack of support for the ABM Treaty and President Reagan's so-called "Star Wars" speech, March 23, 1983, in which he raised the hope of rendering nuclear weapons "impotent and obsolete" through the deployment of strategic defenses, underscore the differences between the present policies and those of the administration's immediate predecessors.

4. See John E. Rielly, editor, *Public Opinion and American Foreign Policy* (Chicago: Chicago Council on Foreign Relations, 1981).

5. See the President's Report to the Congress on Soviet Noncompliance with Arms Control Agreements, (January 23, 1984), pp. 3–4.

6. Ibid., p. 1. After this publication the Reagan administration released the report of the *General Advisory Committee on Arms Control and Disarmament, a Quarter Century of Soviet Compliance Practices under Arms Control Commitments: 1958–1983*. This report cites a long list of Soviet actions considered as material breaches of arms control agreements. These are divided into the following categories: violations of international obligations; breaches of authoritative unilateral commitments; and circumventions.

Chapter 4 (Arms Control: Alliance Cohesion and Extended Deterrence)

1. On the Abandonment-Entrapment Dilemma see Robert Osgood, *NATO: The Entangling Alliance* (Chicago: University of Chicago Press, 1962); Glenn H. Snyder, "The Alliance Security Dilemma," *World Politics*, Vol. XXXVI, No. 4 (July 1984), pp. 461–495; and James L. Richardson, *Germany and the Atlantic Alliance: The Interaction of Strategy and Politics* (Cambridge, MA: Harvard University Press, 1966), especially Part III, NATO Strategy, pp. 135–244.

2. On NATO's nuclear hierarchy, see Jane M. O. Sharp, "Nuclear Weapons and Alliance Cohesion," *Bulletin of the Atomic Scientists*, Vol. 38, No. 6 (July 1982), pp. 33–36.

3. On NATO's nuclear dilemmas see Michael Mandelbaum, "NATO: The Nuclear Alliance," Chapter 6 of *The Nuclear Revolution: International Politics before and after Hiroshima*, (New York: Cambridge University Press, 1981), pp. 147–175; and David N. Schwartz, *NATO's Nuclear Dilemmas* (Washington, D.C.: The Brookings Institution, 1983), especially Chapters I and III.

4. On the background to NATO's double-track decision see Simon Lunn, "The Modernization of NATO's Long Range Theater Nuclear Forces," a report prepared for the United States Congress, House Committee on Foreign Affairs (Washington, D.C.: USGPO, 1980); and Jane M. O. Sharp, "Under-

standing the INF Debacle: Arms Control and Alliance Cohesion," *Arms Control* (London) Vol. 5, No. 2 (September 1984), pp. 95–127.

5. On West European attitudes to the American ABM program in the 1960s see Ian Smart, "Perspectives From Europe," Chapter 7 in Mason Willrich and John B. Rhinelander, editors, *SALT: The Moscow Agreements and Beyond* (New York: The Free Press, 1974), pp. 185–222, at p. 187.

On European apprehension about President Reagan's SDI program, see James M. Markham, "Bonn Is Worried by U.S. Arms Research," *New York Times*, April 14, 1984, p. 3; Christoph Bertram, "The Arms Race in Space: A European Perspective," *Weapons in Space* (New York: W.W. Norton, 1985), fothcoming; Lawrence Freedman, "Europe and the ABM Revival," in Ian Bellamy and Coit Blacker, editors, *Antiballistic Missile Defense in the 1980s* (London: Frank Cass, 1983); David S. Yost, "European Anxieties about Ballistic Missile Defense," *The Washington Quarterly*, Vol. 7, #4 (Fall 1984), pp. 112–129.

6. For McNamara's first attempt to change NATO's doctrine see *Remarks Delivered at a Restricted Session of the NATO Ministerial Meeting (Athens, Greece) May 5, 1962*, released by Freedom of Information Act, August 17, 1979; for the debate on flexible response through the 1960s, see David N. Schwartz, "Flexible Response and the Nuclear Planning Group," in NATO's *Nuclear Dilemmas*, op. cit., pp. 136–192; and Fred Kaplan, *The Wizards of Armageddon* (New York: Simon and Schuster, 1983).

7. For a concise history of efforts to develop guidelines for nuclear use, see J. Michael Legge, *Theater Nuclear Weapons and the NATO Strategy of Flexible Response* R-2964 FF (Santa Monica, CA: Rand Corporation, April 1983). See also Catherine Kelleher, "Thresholds and Theologies: The Need for Critical Reassessment," *Survival*, Vol. XXVI, No. 4 (July/August 1984), pp. 156–163.

8. The concept of a ladder of escalation is from Herman Kahn, *Thinking about the Unthinkable* (New York: Horizon Press, 1962), pp. 177–208.

9. On the problems of trying to refine NATO doctrine, see Christoph Bertram, "Political Implications of the Theater Nuclear Balance," in Barry M. Blechman, editor, *Rethinking the U.S. Strategic Posture* (Cambridge, MA: Ballinger Publishing Company, 1982), pp. 101–128; and Lawrence Freedman, "The No-First-Use Debate and the Theory of Thresholds," in Frank Blackaby et al., editors, *No-First-Use* (London: Taylor Francis for the Stockholm International Peace Research Institute, 1984), pp. 67–78.

10. McGeorge Bundy, George F. Kennan, Robert S. McNamara, and Gerard Smith, "Nuclear Weapons and the Atlantic Alliance," *Foreign Affairs*, Vol. 60, No. 4 (Spring 1982); and the establishment West German response from Karl Kaiser, George Leber, A. Mertes, and Franz-Josef Schulze, "Nuclear Weapons and the Preservation of Peace," *Foreign Affairs*, Vol. 60, No. 5 (Summer 1982).

11. James Martin, "How the Soviet Union Came to Gain Escalation Dominance: Trends and Asymmetries in the Theater Nuclear Balance," Chapter 2 in Uwe Nerlich, editor, *Soviet Power and Western Negotiating Policies*, Vol. 1: *The Soviet Asset: Military Power in the Competition over Europe* (Cambridge, MA: Ballinger Publishing Company, 1983), pp. 89–122.

12. Jane Stromseth, "Prospects for a Conventional Defense of Western Europe: Some Lessons from the 1960s," *Proceedings of the 32nd Pugwash Conference on Science and World Affairs* (Warsaw: August 26–31, 1982), pp. 370–374.

13. William Beecher, *The Boston Globe*, November 10, 1984; "Fee, Fi, Fofa, Hm," *The Economist*, November 24–30, 1984, pp. 47–48; and Bernard Rogers, "Follow on Forces Attack (FOFA): Myths and Realities," *NATO Review*, Vol. 32, #6 (December 1984).

14. See the correspondence on "Conventional Retaliation into Eastern Europe" between Jonathan Dean and Samuel P. Huntington in *International Security*, Vol. 9, No. 1 (Summer 1984), pp. 203–217.

15. Louis P. Halle, *The Cold War as History* (New York: Harper and Row, 1967).

16. Michael MccGwire, "Dilemmas and Delusions of Deterrence," *World Policy Journal*, Vol. 1, No. 4 (Summer 1984), pp. 745–768; and "Deterrence: The Problem not the Solution," *International Affairs*, Vol. 62, #1 (Winter 1985/86), pp. 55–70.

18. For recent analyses of Soviet problems in Eastern Europe see David Holloway and Jane M. O. Sharp, editors, *The Warsaw Pact: Alliance in Transition?* (Ithaca: Cornell University Press, 1984); Sarah Terry, editor, *Soviet Policy in Eastern Europe* (New Haven: Yale University Press, 1984); and Karen Dawisha and Philip Hanson, editors, *Soviet-East European Dilemmas: Coercion, Competition and Consent* (London: Holmes and Meier, 1981).

19. Robert Jervis, *The Illogic of American Nuclear Strategy* (Ithaca: Cornell University Press, 1984); Robert Jervis, "Why Nuclear Superiority Doesn't Matter," *Political Science Quarterly*, Vol. 94, No. 4 (Winter 1979/80); and Glenn H. Snyder, *Deterrence and Defense: Toward a Theory of National Security* (Princeton: Princeton University Press, 1961).

20. Michael MccGwire, "Dilemmas and Delusions of Deterrence," op. cit.

21. Michael Howard, *The Times* (London) November 3, 1981.

22. Paul Huth and Bruce Russett, "What Makes Deterrence Work? Cases from 1900–1980," *World Politics*, Vol. XXXVI, No. 4 (July 1984), pp. 496–526.

23. Earl Ravenal, "Counterforce and Alliance: The Ultimate Connection," *International Security*, Vol. 6, No. 4 (Spring 1982), pp. 26–43; Richard K. Betts, "Elusive Equivalence: The Political and Military Meaning of the Nuclear Balance," in Samuel P. Huntington, *The Strategic Imperative: New Policies for American Security* (Cambridge, MA: Ballinger Publishing Company, 1982), pp. 101–140.

24. John Marshall Lee, "The Use of Nuclear Weapons," a paper presented at the Prospects for Peacemaking Conference, November 29, 1984 (Minneapolis: Hubert Humphrey Institute, 1984) and reproduced (with some changes) as Chapter 2 of this book; and Michael Carver, "No-First-Use: A View from Europe," *Bulletin of the Atomic Scientists*, Vol. 39, No. 3 (March 1983), pp. 22–26.

25. Robert Jervis, *The Illogic of Nuclear Strategy*, op. cit., especially Chapter 6, pp. 147–170.

26. In October 1984 at a MITRE Corporation symposium on national security issues in Bedford, Massachusetts, Richad Garwin suggested that 1,000 nuclear warheads on invulnerable platforms would be a prudent deterrent force for the United States.

27. For a detailed analysis of the range of expert opinion on deterrence theory in the United States, see Charles Glaser, "The Debate over the Requirements of Deterrence," a paper delivered at the Workshop on Explicating the Arms Control Debate, sponsored by the Center for Science and International Affairs, Kennedy School of Government, Harvard University, May 1984.

28. For Denis Healey's deterrence theorem see Bruce Reed and Geoffrey Williams, *Denis Healey and the Policies of Power* (London: Sidgwick and Jackson, 1971), p. 142.

29. Huth and Russett, "What Makes Deterrence Work?" op. cit.

30. Fred Kaplan, "Warring over New Missiles for NATO," *New York Times Magazine*, December 9, 1979; Raymond L. Garthoff, "The NATO Decision Theater Nuclear Forces," *Political Science Quarterly*, Vol. 98, No. 2 (Summer 1983), pp. 197–214.

31. For an authoritative account of the Carter administration's strategic doctrine, see Walter Slocombe, "The Countervailing Strategy," *International Security*, Vol. 5, No. 4 (Spring 1981), pp. 18–27; see also his "Extended Deterrence," in *The Washington Quarterly*, Vol. 4 (Fall 1984), pp. 93–103.

32. In addition to the Gang of Four senior government officials who proposed no-first-use in early 1982, a number of retired senior military officials not only support no-first-use and a nuclear freeze but advocate radical nuclear disarmament measures. These include Canadian Admiral Robert Falls, United States Admirals Noel Gayler and John Marshall Lee, and British Field Marshall Michael Lord Carver.

33. United States Catholic Conference, *The Challenge of Peace: God's Promise and Our Response* (Washington, D.C.: Office of Publishing Series, USCC, 1983).

34. On European public opinion data, see Bruce Russett and Donald R. Deluca, "Theater Nuclear Forces: Public Opinion in Western Europe," *Political Science Quarterly*, Vol. 98, No. 2 (Summer 1983), pp. 179–196; and David Capitanchik, "Public Opinion and Nuclear Weapons in Europe," *Arms Control* (London), Vol. 4, No. 2 (September 1983), pp. 111–133.

35. For analyses comparing American polling data over time see Bernard M. Kramer, S. Michael Kalick, and Michael A. Milburn, "Attitudes Toward Nuclear Weapons and Nuclear War: 1945–1982," *Journal of Social Issues*, Vol. 39, No. 1, 1983; and David Yankelovich et al., *Voter Options on Nuclear Arms Policy* (New York: the Public Agenda Foundation, 1984); see also Daniel Yankelovich and John Doble, "The Public Mood," *Foreign Affairs*, Vol. 63, No. 1 (Fall 1984), pp. 33–46.

36. For arguments advocating the exploitation of new technologies for deep strike missions for NATO conventional forces see the *Report of the European Security Study* (ESECS) *Strengthening Conventional Deterrence in Europe: Proposals*

for the 1980s (New York: St. Martin's Press, 1983). For more thoughtful anal-
yses of the negative implications of deep strike postures for European secu-
rity and stability see Matthew A. Evangelista, "Offense or Defense: A Tale of
Two Commissions," *World Policy Journal*, Vol. 1, No. 1 (Fall 1983), pp. 46–69;
Phil Williams and William Wallace, "Emerging Technologies and European
Security," *Survival*, Vol. XXVI, No. 2 (March/April 1984), pp. 70–78; Joel S.
Witt, "Deep Strike: NATO's New Defense Concept and Its Implications for
Arms Control," *Arms Control Today*, Vol. 13, No. 10 (November 1983); Michael
Klare, paper delivered at the AAAS meeting in New York City (May 1984);
and Fen Osler Hampson, "Groping for Technical Panaceas: The European
Conventional Balance and Nuclear Stability," *International Security*, Vol. 8, No.
3 (Winter 1983/84), pp. 57–82.

37. Jonathan Dean, "Federal Germany after the Euromissiles," *Bulletin of the
Atomic Scientists*, Vol. 39, No. 10 (December 1983), pp. 31–38; and "How to
Lose Germany," *Foreign Policy*, No. 55 (Summer 1984), pp. 54–72.

Chapter 5 (Nuclear Crisis and Human Frailty)

1. Harlan Cleveland, *The Obligations of Power* (New York: Harper and Row,
1966), pp. 35, 51.

2. Henry A. Kissinger, *White House Years* (Boston: Little Brown, 1979).

3. Quoted by V. V. Zhurkin, in *USA and International Political Crises*, Moscow:
Nauka, 1975), p. 12.

4. McGeorge Bundy, "To Cap the Volcano," *Foreign Affairs* (October 1969), p.
10.

5. President's Commission on Strategic Forces, report dated March 21, 1984
(emphasis added).

6. "The Lessons of the Cuban Missile Crisis," *Time*, September 27, 1982, p.
86.

7. Quoted by Adam Ulam, in *Dangerous Relations: The Soviet Union in World
Politics 1970–1982* (New York: Oxford University Press, 1983), p. 85.

8. Dean Acheson, *Present at the Creation* (New York: W. W. Norton, 1969), p.
533.

9. Paul Bracken, *The Command and Control of Nuclear Forces* (New Haven: Yale
University Press, 1983), pp. 41–44.

10. Jack Snyder, "The Soviet Strategic Culture," RAND Report R-2154-AF,
Santa Monica, CA. September 1977.

11. Congressional Research Service, "Authority to Order the Use of Nuclear
Weapons" (Washington: G.P.O., 1977); Department of Defense Directive No.
5100.30 dated December 2, 1971, as amended, pp. 1, 2.

12. DOD Directive No. 5100.30 pp. 1, 4.

13. Lincoln P. Bloomfield, *The Foreign Policy Process: A Modern Primer* (Engle-
wood Cliffs, NJ: Prentice-Hall, 1982), Chapter 3.

14. Scott D. Sagan, "Nuclear Alerts and Crisis Management," *International
Security* (Spring 1985), pp. 134–135.

15. Adm. Gerald E. Miller, "Existing Systems of Command and Control," in Franklyn Griffiths and John C. Polyani, editors, *The Dangers of Nuclear War* (Toronto, 1979), p. 56.

16. U.S. Office of Technology Assessment, MX Missile Basing (Washington: U.S. GPO, 1981), pp. 281–283.

17. Gerald Miller, op.cit., p. 61.

18. Paul Bracken, op.cit., p. 217.

19. Ibid., p. 36.

20. See Lincoln P. Bloomfield, "Reflections on Gaming," *Orbis* (Winter 1984).

21. Memorandum of Understanding between the United States and the U.S.S.R. Regarding the Establishment of a Direct Communication Link, signed June 20, 1963.

22. *New York Times,* June 18, 1984.

23. Desmond Ball, "Can Nuclear War Be Controlled?" Adelphi Paper 169 (London: International Institute for Strategic Studies, 1981), pp. 35–36.

24. Paul Bracken, op.cit., pp. 48, 117–118, 221.

25. Bill Gulley, with Mary Ellen Reese, *Breaking Cover* (New York: Simon and Shuster, 1980), pp. 15, 178, 182–84.

26. Scott Sagan, "Nuclear Alerts and Crisis Management," op.cit.

27. Lt. Gen. William Hilsman, in Hilliard Roderick, editor, *Avoiding Inadvertent War: Crisis Management* (Austin: University of Texas, 1983), p. 36.

28. Robert F. Kennedy, *Thirteen Days: A Memoir of the Cuban Missile Crisis,* (New York: W. W. Norton, 1971), p. 127.

29. Barbara W. Tuchman, *The Guns of August* (New York: Macmillan, 1962), p. 72. See also symposium on World War I in *International Security* (Summer 1984), pp. 3–4, particularly Stephen van Evera, "The Cult of the Offensive. . . ."

30. Henry A. Kissinger, *Time,* October 15, 1979, pp. 71ff.

31. Robert F. Kennedy, op.cit., p. 22.

32. Lincoln P. Bloomfield, *The Foreign Policy Process,* op.cit., Chapter 9.

33. Alexander L. George, *Presidential Decisionmaking in Foreign Policy* (Boulder, CO: Westview Press, 1980), pp. 37, 48. See also Daniel Frei with Christian Catrina, *Risks of Unintended Nuclear War* (Geneva: U.N. Institute for Disarmament Research, 1982), pp. x, 1.

34. Irving L. Janis, *Victims of Groupthink* (Boston: Houghton-Mifflin, 1972), Chapter 1.

35. Joseph de Rivera, *The Psychological Dimension of Foreign Policy* (Columbus, OH: Charles E. Merrill, 1968), p. 252.

36. Robert Jervis, "Hypotheses on Misperception," *World Politics* (April 1968), p. 455.

37. Robert Jervis, "Deterrence and Perception," *International Security* (Winter 1982/83), pp. 20, 28, 252.

38. Robert Mandel, "Political Gaming and Foreign Policy Making during Crises," *World Politics* (July 1977), p. 621.

39. Lynn E. Davis, in Hilliard Roderick, op.cit., p. 73.

40. *Boston Globe,* symposium on anniversary of Cuban Missile Crisis, October 27, 1982.

41. James Thomson, "How Could Vietnam Happen? An Autopsy," *Atlantic Monthly* (April 1968), p. 50.

42. Theodore Sorensen, *Decision-Making in the White House* (New York: Columbia University Press, 1964), p. 76.

43. Thomas C. Weigele, "Decision-Making in an International Crisis: Some Biological Factors," *International Studies Quarterly,* Vol. 17, No. 3 (1973), p. 311.

44. Margaret G. Hermann, "Indicators of Stress in Policymakers during Foreign Policy Crises," *Political Psychology* (Spring 1979), p. 28.

45. Irving L. Janis and Leon Mann, *Decision Making: A Psychological Analysis of Conflict, Choice and Commitment* (New York: The Free Press, 1977), p. 59.

46. Gerald E. Miller, op.cit., p. 62.

47. T. Dobzhansky, quoted by Weigele, op.cit., p. 302.

48. Some, including Harold Brown and Scott Sagan, advocate substituting the vice-president for the president in NEACP.

49. *Wall Street Journal,* December 7, 1983, p. 60.

50. See U.S. Office of Technology Assessment, "Arms Control in Space," Workshop Proceedings, Washington D.C., May 1984, p. 2.

51. See various proposals by Senators Jackson, Nunn, and Warner (press conference, Washington, D.C., April 15, 1982, and Report of Nunn/Warner Working Group on Nuclear Risk Reduction, November 1983, *Survival* (May/June, 1984), pp. 133–35; also William Langer Ury, and Richard Smoke, *Beyond the Hotline: Controlling a Nuclar Crisis, Report to U.S. Arms Control and Disarmament Agency* (Cambridge, MA: Harvard Law School Nuclear Negotiation Project, 1984), and "Improving the Means for Intergovernmental Communications in Crisis," *Survival* (September/October 1984), p. 210.

52. First proposed by the author in *Controlling Small Wars: A Strategy for the 1970s,* with Amelia C. Leiss (New York: Knopf, 1969), p. 412; see also the author's "Spheres of Abstention" in *International Organization* (Summer 1974).

53. For detailed recommendations along these lines see the author's "Reflections on Gaming," op. cit.

About the Authors

Lincoln P. Bloomfield is Professor of Political Science at Massachusetts Institute of Technology. He has served in the U. S. Navy, State Department and National Security Council.

Harlan Cleveland is Professor of Public Affairs and Dean of the Hubert H. Humphrey Institute of Public Affairs at the University of Minnesota. He has been Assistant Secretary of State and U. S. Ambassador to NATO.

John Marshall Lee is Vice Admiral (retired) in the U.S. Navy. He has been Assistant Director of the Arms Control and Disarmament Agency.

Michael Nacht is Professor of Public Affairs and Acting Dean of the School of Public Affairs at the University of Maryland.

Dean Rusk is Professor of International Law at the University of Georgia. He was Secretary of State under Presidents John F. Kennedy and Lyndon B. Johnson from 1961 to 1969.

Jane M. O. Sharp is a Senior Research Fellow at SIPRI, Stockholm International Peace Research Institute.

Marshall Shulman is former Director of the W. Averell Harriman Institute for the Advanced Study of the Soviet Union at Columbia University, also Ambassador-at-Large for Soviet Affairs in the State Department.

Index